Exalting Christ...
The Lamb of God

A Study of John 15-21

FROM THE BIBLE-TEACHING MINISTRY OF

Charles R. Swindoll

INSIGHT FOR LIVING

Charles R. Swindoll graduated in 1963 from Dallas Theological Seminary, where he now serves as the school's fourth president, helping to prepare a new generation of men and women for the ministry. Chuck has served in pastorates in three states: Massachusetts, Texas, and California, including almost twenty-three years at the First Evangelical Free Church in Fullerton, California. He is currently senior pastor of Stonebriar Community Church in Frisco, Texas, north of Dallas. His sermon messages have been aired over radio since 1979 as the *Insight for Living* broadcast. A best-selling author, he has written numerous books and booklets on many subjects.

Editor in Chief:
Cynthia Swindoll
Coauthor of Text:
Ken Gire
Author of Living Insights, Senior Editor, and Assistant Writer:
Wendy Peterson
Editors:
Christina Grimstad
Karla Lenderink
Copy Editor:
Marco Salazar

Rights and Permissions:
The Meredith Agency
Graphic System Administrator:
Bob Haskins
Director, Communications Division:
John Norton
Print Production Manager:
Don Bernstein
Project Coordinator:
Jennifer Hubbard
Printer:
Sinclair Printing Company

Unless otherwise identified, all Scripture references are from the New American Standard Bible, copyright © The Lockman Foundation 1960, 1962, 1963, 1968, 1971, 1972, 1973, 1975, 1977. Used by permission. Scripture taken from the Holy Bible, New International Version, Copyright © 1973, 1978, 1984 International Bible Society, used by permission of Zondervan Bible Publishers [NIV].

In chapter 6, "Divine Intercession," and chapter 7, "When Jesus Prayed for You," unless otherwise identified, all Scripture references are from the New American Standard Bible, updated edition, copyright © The Lockman Foundation 1960, 1962, 1963, 1968, 1971, 1972, 1973, 1975, 1977, 1995. Used by permission.

Based on the outlines, charts and transcripts of Charles R. Swindoll's sermons, the study guide titled *Beholding Christ . . . The Lamb of God* was renamed in 2000 to *Exalting Christ . . . The Lamb of God* and the text was revised by Wendy Peterson, senior editor and assistant writer in the Educational Ministries Department of Insight for Living:

Copyright © 2000 by Insight for Living

Guide titled *Beholding Christ . . . The Lamb of God* coauthored by Ken Gire:
Copyright © 1987 by Charles R. Swindoll, Inc.

Outlines published by New Standard for Living and Insight for Living titled *The Gospel of John:*
Copyright © 1975, 1976 by Charles R. Swindoll, Inc.

Original outlines, charts, and transcripts for series titled *The Gospel of John:*
Copyright © 1975, 1976 by Charles R. Swindoll, Inc.

An effort has been made to locate sources and obtain permission where necessary for the quotations used in this book. In the event of any unintentional omission, a modification will gladly be incorporated in future printings.

ISBN 1-57972-330-6
Cover design by Michael Standlee Design
Cover image © Stephen Simpson/FPG International LLC
Printed in the United States of America

Contents

Introduction

John the Baptizer once introduced Christ as "the Lamb of God who takes away the sin of the world." Vivid words . . . true words.

In these concluding seven chapters of the Gospel of John, the Lamb is on display. After an intimate gathering with His men at their last supper together, He faces the horrors of six illegal trials, scourging, crucifixion, and death. The Lamb is slain. But the Lamb is later raised!

Even though some of this information is familiar to many Christians, we never tire of exalting the Lamb. I am delighted to know that you will be focusing your attention upon Him during these days. I hope each lesson will deepen your devotion for Christ, who accomplished our salvation at the cross . . . having been raised from the dead on our behalf.

Chuck Swindoll

Chuck Swindoll

Putting Truth Into Action

Knowledge apart from application falls short of God's desire for His children. He wants us to apply what we learn so that we will change and grow. This study guide was prepared with these goals in mind. As you go through the following pages, we hope your desire to discover biblical truth will grow as your understanding of God's Word increases, and that you will be encouraged to apply what you've learned.

To assist you in your study, we've included a section called 🔖**Living Insights** at the end of each lesson. These exercises will challenge you to study further and to think of specific ways to put your discoveries into action.

There are many ways to use this guide—in personal devotions, group studies, discussions with friends and family, and Sunday school classes. And, of course, it's an ideal study aid when you're listening to its corresponding *Insight for Living* radio series.

To benefit most from this study guide, we would encourage you to consider it a spiritual journal. That's why we've included space in the **Living Insights** for recording your thoughts and discoveries. We hope you'll return to those sections often for review and encouragement as you continue to grow in your walk with Christ.

Insight for Living

Exalting Christ...
The Lamb of God

A STUDY OF JOHN 15-21

JOHN

	Deity	God-Man	Ministry	Discourse	Trials and Death	Empty Tomb	Assurance
	"The Word was God." (1:1)	"The Word became flesh." (1:14)					
		Miraculous signs: Water into wine (2) Heals official's son (4)	*Miraculous signs:* Heals invalid at Bethesda (5) Feeds 5,000 (6) Walks on water (6) Heals blind man (9) Raises Lazarus (11)	*Private talks:* Servanthood (13) Heaven (14) Abiding (15) Promises (16) Prayer (17)	✝	*Private talks:* Appearances (20)	*Private talks:* Future (21)
							EPILOGUE
Stage	CHAPTER 1:1–13	CHAPTERS 1:14–4:54	CHAPTERS 5–12	CHAPTERS 13–17	CHAPTERS 18–19	CHAPTER 20	CHAPTER 21
	Prologue	Acceptance	Conflict	Preparation	Crucifixion	Triumph	
Audience	Public message		CHANGE	Private message			
Time	Three years			Several days			
Jesus' Seven "I Am" Statements	• "I am the bread of life." (6:35) • "I am the Light of the world." (8:12) • "I am the door." (10:9) • "I am the good shepherd." (10:11)			• "I am the resurrection and the life." (11:25) • "I am the way, and the truth, and the life." (14:6) • "I am the true vine." (15:1)			
Main Theme and Key Verse	"These have been written so that you may believe that Jesus is the Christ, the Son of God; and that believing you may have life in His name." (20:31)						

Chapter 1

Abiding

John 15:1–11

As we begin our study of this last section in John's Gospel, it's essential to remember where we are in Jesus' life.

In a matter of hours, He will be dead, nailed to a Roman cross.

The disciples have prepared the Passover lamb, but now the Lamb of God prepares His disciples for the ultimate Passover to which the ancient feast has long looked in hope (see Luke 22:7–8; 1 Cor. 5:7b; 1 Pet. 1:18–20). In an act of humble love, Jesus has washed their feet, giving His men an example of self-sacrificing service (John 13:1–17)— a picture that will be carried to extreme fulfillment on the cross.

One disciple, whose feet were also washed by Jesus and to whom the Lord offered every chance of grace, has already fled into the night, into the deep darkness of Satan's realm. Judas has turned his back on the Light of the World and run to the benighted religious authorities to finalize the arrangements for Jesus' betrayal (vv. 18–30).

What is Jesus' response to this impending danger and the approaching horror of crucifixion? Is it panic, self-absorption, a desperate plan for escape? No, His focus is on returning to the Father with redemption in His hand for all who will believe in Him. And, characteristically, His attention is on the needs of others—His remaining eleven disciples, who are anxious, fearful, and confused about what will happen to them when He is gone.

Listen to His gentle voice as He calms their troubled hearts, reassures them of His presence through His Spirit, and instructs them in the way of His life.

> "If I then, the Lord and the Teacher, washed your feet, you also ought to wash one another's feet." (v. 14)

1

"A new commandment I give to you, that you love one an-other, even as I have loved you, that you also love one an-other. By this all men will know that you are My disciples, if you have love for one another." (vv. 34–35)

"Let not your heart be troubled; believe in God, believe also in Me." (14:1)

"In My Father's house are many dwelling places . . . I go to pre-pare a place for you. . . . I will come again, and receive you to Myself; that where I am, there you may be also." (vv. 2–3)

"I am the way, and the truth, and the life; no one comes to the Father, but through Me." (v. 6)

"I will ask the Father, and He will give you another Helper, that He may be with you forever." (v. 16)

"I will not leave you as orphans; I will come to you." (v. 18)

"Peace I leave with you; My peace I give to you; not as the world gives, do I give to you. Let not your heart be troubled, nor let it be fearful." (v. 27)

In His next words, recorded in John 15, Jesus explains to His friends how they can always be together. Nothing can separate them, not even death, because love will bridge the distance between heaven and earth.

I. General Survey of John 15

Chapter 15 is a continuation of Jesus' Upper Room Discourse (John 13–17), and it addresses the most important relationships a Chris-tian must maintain. Verses 1–11 deal with the believer's relation-ship with Christ. The key term in this section of the chapter is *abide*; used ten times in these eleven verses, it emphasizes *union*. Verses 12–17 focus on the believer's relationship with other be-lievers. *Love* is the key word in this section, used four times in the six verses; the emphasis here is on *communion*. Finally, verses 18–27 highlight the believer's relationship with the world. The key word is *hate*, used eight times in just ten verses. The emphasis of this last section is on *disunion*.

II. Specific Study of John 15:1–11

With our focus on our relationship with Christ, let's now examine verses 1–11 in greater detail.

A. Observations. Four key observations will help us get a better grasp on the meaning of what Jesus is saying.

1. This entire passage is for believers only. Jesus is talking intimately with His disciples, not the multitudes. His words are aimed at those who have already established a relationship with Him (see v. 3).

2. **The verses revolve around a metaphor.** The visual picture of the vine and branches tells us that the central idea is *vital union.* Also, just as the eagle and the stars and stripes are well-known American symbols, so the vineyard would have presented a familiar image to the Jews (compare Ps. 80:8–17; Isa. 5:1–7; Jer. 2:21; Ezek. 15; 19:10–14; Hos. 10:1).

3. **The main subject is abiding.** Jesus uses the image of fruit, not that of a seed taking root. The thrust of His teaching, therefore, is not on becoming a Christian but on becoming a *productive* Christian.

4. **The result of abiding is fruit bearing.** Scan the passage and note how frequently the word *fruit* is used: "does not bear fruit" (John 15:2a); "bears fruit" (v. 2b); "bear more fruit" (v. 2c); "cannot bear fruit of itself" (v. 4); "bears much fruit" (v. 5); "bear much fruit" (v. 8).

B. **Interpretation.** In the picture Jesus paints, three symbols stand out: the vine, the vinedresser, and the branch.

"I am the true vine, and My Father is the vinedresser. Every branch in Me that does not bear fruit, He takes away; and every branch that bears fruit, He prunes it, that it may bear more fruit. You are already clean because of the word which I have spoken to you. Abide in Me, and I in you. As the branch cannot bear fruit of itself, unless it abides in the vine, so neither can you, unless you abide in Me." (vv. 1–4)

1. **The vine.** In the last of His "I am" statements, Jesus identifies Himself as the genuine Vine—the only source of spiritual life. He is the One responsible for the fruit which we, as Christians, bear. Many view the fruit in John 15 as souls won through evangelism, but it can also refer to love and obedience, as well as character qualities of Christlikeness, namely, the fruit of the spirit: love, joy, peace, patience, kindness, goodness, faithfulness, gentleness, self-control (Gal. 5:22–23; see also 2 Pet. 1:5–7). In short, the fruit "is the life of Jesus himself reproduced in the lives of the disciples in the midst of the life of the world."[1]

---

1. Lesslie Newbigin, *The Light Has Come: An Exposition of the Fourth Gospel* (Grand Rapids, Mich.: William B. Eerdmans Publishing Co., 1982), p. 197.

2. The vinedresser. God the Father is pictured here as a busy, active, faithful gardener working in His vineyard—an image already well-established in the Old Testament. Sadly, however, His vine—Israel—failed to produce the good fruit He had cultivated it for:

> Let me sing now for my well-beloved
> A song of my beloved concerning His vineyard.
> My well-beloved had a vineyard on a fertile hill.
> And He dug it all around, removed its stones,
> And planted it with the choicest vine.
> And He built a tower in the middle of it,
> And hewed out a wine vat in it;
> Then He expected it to produce good grapes,
> But it produced only worthless ones.
> "And now, O inhabitants of Jerusalem and men
>   of Judah,
> Judge between Me and My vineyard.
> What more was there to do for My vineyard
>   that I have not done in it?
> Why, when I expected it to produce good
>   grapes did it produce worthless ones? . . ."
> For the vineyard of the Lord of hosts is the
>   house of Israel,
> And the men of Judah His delightful plant.
> Thus He looked for justice, but behold,
>   bloodshed;
> For righteousness, but behold, a cry of
>   distress. (Isa. 5:1–4, 7)

Jesus undoubtedly had this passage in mind when He talked of Himself as being "the true vine" who fulfilled "what God had intended for Israel"[2] and of His Father as being the Vinedresser. In John 15:2, Jesus reveals two actions of the Vinedresser: (1) He does something with the branch that isn't bearing any fruit at all; (2) He does something with the branch that is already bearing fruit. In the first case, He "takes away"; in the second, He "prunes." Vines occasionally yield an unproductive, fruitless branch. When that happens, the gardener immediately goes to work, as Merrill Tenney notes in his commentary.

2. Edwin A. Blum, "John," in *The Bible Knowledge Commentary,* New Testament edition, ed. John F. Walvoord and Roy B. Zuck (Colorado Springs, Colo.: Chariot Victor Publishing, 1983), p. 325.

Viticulture . . . consists mainly of pruning. In pruning a vine, two principles are generally observed: first, all dead wood must be ruthlessly removed; and second, the live wood must be cut back drastically. Dead wood harbors insects and disease and may cause the vine to rot, to say nothing of being unproductive and unsightly. Live wood must be trimmed back in order to prevent such heavy growth that the life of the vine goes into the wood rather than into fruit. The vineyards in the early spring look like a collection of barren, bleeding stumps; but in the fall they are filled with luxuriant purple grapes. As the farmer wields the pruning knife on his vines, so God cuts dead wood out from among His saints, and often cuts back the living wood so far that His method seems cruel. Nevertheless, from those who have suffered the most there often comes the greatest fruitfulness.[3]

The Pain of Being Pruned

For the plant, pruning is never a pleasant experience. Yet without it, the vine would wind up a tangle of unproductive overgrowth.

Is God pruning your life now? If so, it can be a painful process, and you will probably bleed more sap than you will produce fruit. But if your branches are smarting from the sharp swings of God's pruning hook, take hope. Just as there is a time to be pruned, so there is a time to be productive. And that is only a short growing season away!

3. **The branch.** Jesus uses the figure of the branch to depict the Christian. In verse 2, He makes an important distinction between our position in the Vine, which is Christ, and our production. The difference is seen when comparing verse 2 with verse 4: "Every branch in Me" speaks of our position in Christ; "Abide in Me" is a command given to those who are already branches. This distinction

3. Merrill C. Tenney, *John: The Gospel of Belief* (Grand Rapids, Mich.: William B. Eerdmans Publishing Co., 1948), pp. 227–28.

separates the two activities of the believer—the direct responsibility of abiding: our *position* (v. 4); and the indirect response of bearing fruit: our *production* (v. 5). Note that the command is not to produce fruit but to abide. When we are abiding, fruit comes naturally. The fruit in view here is not produced by the branch but by the Vine itself. Without abiding, a branch cannot produce even a bud of real fruit.

> "I am the vine, you are the branches; he who
> abides in Me, and I in him, he bears much fruit;
> for apart from Me you can do nothing." (v. 5)

Nothing? That's right, nothing . . . at least nothing of genuine or eternal value. Whatever you produce in your life that is not an outgrowth of a vital relationship with Christ is like plastic fruit. It looks good from a distance but can't bear up under the close scrutiny of eternity. And what about the far-reaching effects of not abiding? Verse 6 describes the consequences.

> "If anyone does not abide in Me, he is thrown
> away as a branch, and dries up; and they
> gather them, and cast them into the fire, and
> they are burned."

If we abide in Christ, we bear fruit; if we don't, we become barren. And as a barren branch, we become useless to those around us, either for shade or for nourishment. When the vineyard is in this condition, the Vinedresser comes in and cleans it up with His disciplinary hand. Some interpret this to mean we can lose our salvation. But more likely, it's not our salvation we lose (which would contradict many Scripture passages: see John 3:16, 36; 5:24; 10:28–29; Rom. 8:1) but our rewards. The Father does not put the branch in the fire but the works done in the power of the flesh. Note that the plural *them* could not refer to the singular *branch*. Logically, it must refer to the works done in the flesh by the believer. And it is these works—not the believer—that are burned up.[4] Paul

---

4. Many respected commentators offer a third interpretation of who the branches are that are thrown away and burned (v. 6): "The 'burned' branches refer to professing Christians who, like Judas, are not genuinely saved and therefore are judged. Like a dead branch, a person without Christ is spiritually dead and therefore will be punished in eternal fire (cf. Matt. 25:46). Judas was with Jesus; he seemed like a 'branch.' But he did not have God's life in him; therefore he departed; his destiny was like that of a dead branch" (compare John 13:2, 10–11; 15:3). Blum, "John," in *The Bible Knowledge Commentary*, pp. 325–26. See also Bruce B. Barton, Philip W. Comfort, David R. Veerman, and Neil Wilson, *John*, Life Application Bible Commentary

conveys the same truth through a different metaphor in 1 Corinthians 3:12–15.

Now if any man builds upon the foundation with gold, silver, precious stones, wood, hay, straw, each man's work will become evident; for the day will show it, because it is to be revealed with fire; and the fire itself will test the quality of each man's work. If any man's work which he has built upon it remains, he shall receive a reward. If any man's work is burned up, he shall suffer loss; but he himself shall be saved, yet so as through fire.

Most of our lives are mixtures of wood, hay, and straw, along with gold, silver, and precious stones. The former, God destroys; the latter, He blesses. John 15:7–11 delineates those blessings. The first is that *prayer is answered.*

"If you abide in Me, and My words abide in you, ask whatever you wish, and it shall be done for you." (v. 7)

The second is that *God is glorified.*

"By this is My Father glorified, that you bear much fruit, and so prove to be My disciples." (v. 8)

The third is that *your life will be motivated by love.*

"Just as the Father has loved Me, I have also loved you; abide in My love. If you keep My commandments, you will abide in My love; just as I have kept My Father's commandments, and abide in His love." (vv. 9–10)

The fourth is that *joy will be yours in abundance.* Like a flag that flies over the castle when the king is on the throne, so joy will stand over your life as a testimony that Jesus reigns in your heart.

Series (Wheaton, Ill.: Tyndale House Publishers, 1993), pp. 307, 309–10; D. A. Carson, *The Gospel according to John* (Grand Rapids, Mich.: William B. Eerdmans Publishing Co., 1991), pp. 515, 517, 519; William Hendriksen, *Exposition of the Gospel According to John,* New Testament Commentary Series, two volumes in one (Grand Rapids, Mich.: Baker Book House, 1954), vol. 2, p. 301; Bruce Milne, *The Message of John: Here Is Your King!,* The Bible Speaks Today Series (Downers Grove, Ill.: InterVarsity Press, 1993), pp. 220–21; Leon Morris, *The Gospel according to John,* rev. ed., The New International Commentary on the New Testament Series (Grand Rapids, Mich.: William B. Eerdmans Publishing Co., 1995), p. 594, fn. 10; Merrill C. Tenney, "The Gospel of John," in *The Expositor's Bible Commentary,* gen. ed. Frank E. Gaebelein (Grand Rapids, Mich.: Zondervan Publishing House, 1981), vol. 9, pp. 151–52.

"These things I have spoken to you, that My
joy may be in you, and that your joy may be
made full." (v. 11)

III. Practical and Personal Summary

Two important truths stem from this study: first, *refusing to abide
results in barrenness;* and second, *abiding results in fruitfulness.*
Abiding in Christ should be as natural as a tree abiding in the
soil—and as necessary! When the tree faithfully abides in that soil,
fruit is the inevitable result. And like the person who abides in the
Word, as described by the psalmist, so is the person who abides
in Christ.

And he will be like a tree firmly planted by streams of
water,
Which yields its fruit in its season,
And its leaf does not wither;
And in whatever he does, he prospers. (Ps. 1:3)

Living Insights

Well, you've read a lot about the Vine, the Vinedresser, branches,
pruning, and bearing fruit. Take some time now to pray, asking God
to help you sift through all that you've read and make crystal-clear
what He sent His Son to say. With the Lord's guidance, reread John
15:1–11, perhaps in a different translation than what was used in
this study. Then reflect on the following questions.

What does it mean to abide in Christ (see vv. 7a, 10)?

_____

_____

_____

_____

How does obeying Christ show our love for Him? What is the
relationship between love and obedience (see 13:34–35; 14:15, 21,
23–24, 31; 15:9)?

_____

_____

_____

_____

What is Jesus' love for us like (13:1, 4–5, 13–17; 14:3, 13–14, 18, 21, 27; 15:9, 11, 13, 15)?

_____

_____

_____

What will the fruit from Christ's kind of love look like? How might it be different from the world's love?

_____

_____

_____

What is the goal of the fruit we are to bear (15:8)? How do our love for and obedience to Christ accomplish this?

_____

_____

_____

How should Christ's direction to abide in His love and bear much fruit shape our prayers? When He promises, "Ask whatever you wish, and it shall be done for you" (v. 7), is that a blanket promise to fulfill our every wish? Why or why not? How does verse 8 inform your answer?

_____

_____

_____

Eugene Peterson observes that "when we abide in Christ, our prayers cease to be disguised efforts to increase personal possessions and power, and become the means of being increased in Christ."[5] In other words, we're less concerned with building little earthly kingdoms of our own and more intent on building up the

---

5. Eugene H. Peterson, _Forces Concealed in Quiet: Meditations from the Writings of John the Apostle_ (Nashville, Tenn.: Thomas Nelson Publishers, 1985), no. 154.

kingdom of heaven. Our fruitfulness, too, is less about showing what good people we are and more about making Christ's life visible and touchable to a world that needs Him.

How are you doing at abiding with Christ? Is He the focus of your heart, not just a hub around which your activities swirl? Are you letting His kind of love be the shaper of your life?

_____

_____

_____

_____

What kind of fruit is your life bearing? What would you like to see that isn't there yet?

_____

_____

_____

_____

How balanced is your prayer life between God's mission in this world and your personal needs and wants?

_____

_____

_____

_____

If you're not quite where you'd like to be, don't beat up on yourself. That's not what Christ wants at all. Rather, take your concerns to Him and ask for His help. He gives it graciously (see Heb. 4:14–16; James 1:5). And remember His goal:

"These things I have spoken to you, that My joy may be in you, and that your joy may be made full." (John 15:11)

Final Week: From Public To Private

According to John's Gospel

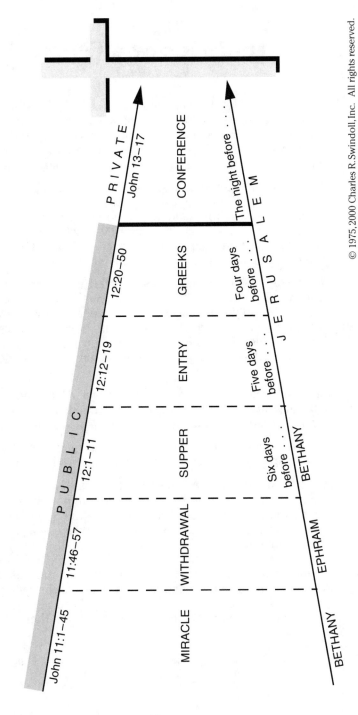

John 11:1–45	11:46–57	12:1–11	12:12–19	12:20–50	John 13–17
MIRACLE	WITHDRAWAL	SUPPER	ENTRY	GREEKS	CONFERENCE
		Six days before . . .	Five days before . . .	Four days before . . .	The night before . . .

PUBLIC — PRIVATE

BETHANY — EPHRAIM — BETHANY — JERUSALEM

11

Chapter 2
Qualities of a Friend
John 15:12–17

Born of older parents in eighteenth-century Devonshire, England, the famous poet Samuel Taylor Coleridge was a lonely genius. His father died when he was nine years old, and a year later Coleridge was sent to London to live with his uncle. There he entered the charity school of Christ's Hospital, taking refuge in books as his only friends.

At nineteen, he entered Cambridge, where his career interests vacillated between medicine, philosophy, and writing. He quickly distinguished himself as a scholar and gained notoriety as a poet, critic, and playwright. Even in his twenties, Coleridge lectured extensively on Shakespeare and Milton. Many of his poems—such as "The Nightingale," "Kubla Kahn," and the "Rime of the Ancient Mariner"—became classics.

But none of these achievements satisfied the emptiness in his heart for friendship. By the age of twenty-four, he had turned to drugs to deaden the resounding loneliness. His only deep friendships were with fellow poet William Wordsworth and later with physician James Gillman, who cared for Coleridge in his early forties. For the last eighteen years of his life, years that in many ways were his happiest, Coleridge rarely left the Gillman home.

Many of Coleridge's works dwell on misery and tragedy . . . except for one poem written shortly before his death, titled "Youth and Age." The second stanza cradles the moving line: "Friendship is a sheltering tree."[1]

In the gray twilight of his life, Coleridge recognized something that genius, popularity, and money could never replace—the value of a friend.

I. A Study of the Second Section of John 15
When death nears, it is remarkable how important the shade of our sheltering friends becomes. Not even the Son of God wanted to be alone when the shadow of the Cross darkened His last days. At that time, more than any other, He wanted to be surrounded by His most intimate friends. And with those friends Jesus shared the innermost feelings of His heart in what is known as the Upper Room Discourse. In this chapter, we will look at the second section of John 15, verses 12–17, where Christ discusses the love and communion believers should have with one another.

---

1. As quoted in *Bartlett's Familiar Quotations,* 14th ed., rev. and enl., ed. Emily Morison Beck (Boston, Mass.: Little, Brown and Co., 1980), p. 527.

A. Transitional connection: the command. Jesus has just told His disciples that His instructions are for their joy (v. 11). What instructions has He given them? "If you keep My commandments, you will abide in My love; just as I have kept My Father's commandments, and abide in His love" (v. 10). And His "new commandment," as we saw in chapter 13, was to love each other as Jesus has loved us (vv. 34–35). Now in chapter 15, He reiterates and reemphasizes what He wants to characterize the new life He will secure for us on the Cross: "This is My commandment, that you love one another, just as I have loved you. . . . This I command you, that you love one another." (vv. 12, 17)

   1. The content. The verb in verse 12 is in the present tense. It indicates ongoing action: "keep on loving one another." Jesus' point is that love is not to be a sporadic, impulsive, or capricious outburst of emotion; it is to be a sustained, intense, and committed outworking of the will. Love is not a Christmas feeling that bubbles to the surface when circumstances are conducive; it is a decision to continually seek the highest good of others. Its roots are not in humanism or in Hollywood but in heaven. We aren't to love others on the basis of their inherent goodness or external attractiveness but on the basis of the example Jesus set for us.

   2. The comparison. Up until this time, Scripture has taught us to love our neighbors as ourselves (Lev. 19:18; Luke 10:27). Our love for ourselves has been the basis of comparison for our love for others. But now Jesus gives the disciples a new commandment based on a different point of comparison. They are to love one another "just as I have loved you." Jesus loved the disciples unconditionally. He loved them in their unbelief (Matt. 14:31); He loved them in their pettiness (18:1–6). He loved them in their desertion (26:31–32); He loved them in their denial (26:33–34); He loved them in their betrayal (26:47–50). And He loved them to the end (John 13:1). Jesus could continually love the disciples because He continually abided in the Father, vitally linked in unbroken fellowship. Now as we come to John 15:13, we see their relationship with Jesus move to a deeper level—beyond discipleship to friendship.

B. Essential characteristics: the qualities. As He introduces this new level of relating, Jesus makes the qualities of a friend visible by detailing four massive limbs of that "sheltering tree."

1. Disregard for personal sacrifice. The first branch of the tree is found in verse 13.

> "Greater love has no one than this, that one lay down his life for his friends."

The primary interpretation of verse 13 refers to Christ laying down His life for the disciples. But on a secondary level, there's a principle that relates to friendship. When you have a friend, you will disregard the pain of personal sacrifice—even if that sacrifice is death.

Greater Love, No Greater Friend

Charles Dickens' *Tale of Two Cities* presents a classic illustration of John 15:13. Set during the French Revolution, it is the story of two friends, Charles Darnay and Sydney Carton. Darnay is a young Frenchman who has been thrown in a dungeon to await the guillotine. Carton is a wasted English lawyer whose life has been one of careless reprobation.

In a beautiful allegory of Christ's atonement for us, Carton slips into the dungeon and exchanges clothes with the prisoner, allowing Darnay to escape. The next morning, Sydney Carton makes his way up the steps that lead to the guillotine. His final words are triumphant:

> "I see the lives for which I lay down my life, peaceful, useful, prosperous and happy, in that England which I shall see no more. . . . It is a far, far better thing that I do, than I have ever done; it is a far, far better rest that I go to than I have ever known."[2]

That is true friendship. That is the love Jesus demonstrated to His disciples—and offers to you and me (Rom. 5:8). No wonder the hymn says, "What a friend we have in Jesus."

---

2. Dedication to mutual aims. The second large limb in friendship's sheltering tree is found in verse 14.

> "You are My friends, if you do what I command you."

---

2. Charles Dickens, *A Tale of Two Cities* (Garden City, N.Y.: Nelson Doubleday, n.d.), pp. 350–51.

The present tense here—meaning "keep on doing"—tells us that friendship depends on common aims and outlook. As commentator Leon Morris observes,

> Once again obedience is the test of discipleship. The friends of Jesus are those who habitually obey him.[3]

Jesus' goals, then, became those of His disciples, revealing the friendship that existed between them. We find another example of this quality in the friendship between Paul and Timothy.

> But I hope in the Lord Jesus to send Timothy to you shortly, so that I also may be encouraged when I learn of your condition. For I have no one else of kindred spirit who will genuinely be concerned for your welfare. For they all seek after their own interests, not those of Christ Jesus. But you know of his proven worth that he served with me in the furtherance of the gospel like a child serving his father. (Phil. 2:19–22)

We see two important things in these verses: a statement and an analogy. Verse 20 contains the statement: "I have no one else of *kindred* spirit." The Greek word, used only here in all the New Testament, literally means "equal soul" or "like soul." Aristotle once said: "A true friend is one soul in two bodies."[4] That is how close Paul and Timothy were—with a one-souled quality only true friends have. In verse 22, we find the analogy: "He served with me in the furtherance of the gospel like a child serving his father." In friendship there's a union of philosophy, a mutuality of aims and objectives, a like-mindedness, a kinship of souls.

3. **Discussion of privileged information.** A third bough branching in friendship's sheltering tree grows from verse 15 of John 15.

> "No longer do I call you slaves, for the slave does not know what his master is doing; but I have called you friends, for all things that I have heard from My Father I have made known to you."

---

3. Leon Morris, *The Gospel according to John,* rev. ed., The New International Commentary on the New Testament Series (Grand Rapids, Mich.: William B. Eerdmans Publishing Co., 1995), p. 599.

4. *Five Thousand Quotations for All Occasions,* ed. Lewis C. Henry (Garden City, N.Y.: Doubleday and Co., 1945), p. 101.

D. A. Carson explains the great honor Jesus is bestowing on His disciples.

An absolute potentate demands obedience in all his subjects. His slaves, however, are simply told what to do, while his friends are informed of his thinking, enjoy his confidence and learn to obey with a sense of privilege and with full understanding of their master's heart. So also here: Jesus' absolute right to command is in no way diminished, but he takes pains to inform his friends of his motives, plans, purposes. . . . In times past God's covenant people were not informed of God's saving plan in the full measure now accorded Jesus' disciples. Although there is much they cannot grasp (16:12), within that constraint Jesus has told them everything he has learned from his Father. The Paraclete [Holy Spirit] whom Jesus sends will in the wake of the cross and resurrection complete the revelation bound up with the person and work of Christ (14:26; 16:12–15), thereby making Jesus' disciples more informed, more privileged, more comprehending than any believers who ever came before.[5]

When we apply this to a strictly human plane, we see that open sharing, no hiding, and intimate depth mark close friendships. Real friendship is marked by the sharing of soul secrets, which means that it is not public information traded on the lips of indiscreet onlookers. It is shared in private with a select, trusted few.

Friends of the King

The courts of eastern kings held an elite group of men called "friends of the king." They had unrestricted access to the monarch. Having the right even to come into the king's bedchamber, they often met with him informally before he saw his political, economic, or military advisors.

Think about the incredible offer Jesus gives—to

---

5. D. A. Carson, *The Gospel according to John* (Grand Rapids, Mich.: William B. Eerdmans Publishing Co., 1991), p. 523.

be no longer slaves but friends. We need no longer
gaze at Him from afar. We are no longer excluded
from His intimate circle of confidants. Friends! Incredible, but true.

4. Desire to implement fulfillment. Jesus' next words are
reminiscent of the Lord's reminder to His people Israel
when they were about to enter the Promised Land:

"For you are a holy people to the Lord your
God; the Lord your God has chosen you to be
a people for His own possession out of all the
peoples who are on the face of the earth. The
Lord did not set His love on you nor choose
you because you were more in number than
any of the peoples, for you were the fewest of
all peoples, but because the Lord loved you."
(Deut. 7:6–8a)

Likewise, Jesus asserts that He takes the initiative in
choosing and consecrating His disciples to live out the
New Covenant He will achieve on the Cross and at the
empty tomb:

"You did not choose Me, but I chose you, and
appointed you, that you should go and bear
fruit, and that your fruit should remain, that
whatever you ask of the Father in My name,
He may give to you." (John 15:16)

In His great grace, Jesus has chosen and appointed us to
be productive in sharing His mission and bringing glory
to His Father. He will even provide what we need to accomplish this, which, as Bruce Milne notes, is the "ultimate encouragement" of His grace:

We go, not because we are worthy, or equipped,
or attractive, or skilled, or experienced, or in
any way suitable and appropriate. We go because we have been summoned and sent.
Since he has called us he will equip and enable
us for our witness. As with Israel his choice is
with a view to service. We are chosen to *go
and bear fruit*.[6]

---

6. Bruce Milne, *The Message of John: Here Is Your King!*, The Bible Speaks Today Series (Downers
Grove, Ill.: InterVarsity Press, 1993), p. 223.

What lesson can we glean from Jesus' words for our personal relationships? That nothing is more exciting than seeing a close friend succeed. This should be the purpose of our relationships—to help each other reach maximum fulfillment in what Christ has chosen and sent us to do and to be.

II. A Summary of Today's Insights on Friendship

Before you walk away from this study, fix two truths in your mind. One, a sheltering tree bears the fruit of security, confidence, care, and encouragement. Two, a sheltering tree has roots that abide. Friendship lends warmth and meaning to life. Let's not live in such a way that Coleridge's self-written epitaph might apply to us:

Beneath this sod
A poet lies, or that which once seemed he—
Oh, lift a thought in prayer for S.T.C.!
That he, who many a year, with toil of breath,
Found death in life, may here find life in death.[7]

Let's live our lives under the sheltering tree of Christ's friendship, where the fruit from His spreading branches can nourish and refresh us forever.

Living Insights

One thing will impact our ability to love one another like nothing else. What is that? Our ability to receive Christ's love for us. This is why the apostle Paul knelt before God, the "magnificent Father

who parcels out all heaven and earth. I ask him to strengthen you by his Spirit—not a brute strength but a glorious inner strength—that Christ will live in you as you open the door and invite him in. And I ask him that with both feet planted firmly on love, you'll be able to take in with all Christians the extravagant dimensions of Christ's love. Reach out and experience the breadth! Test its length! Plumb the depths! Rise to the heights! Live full lives, full in the fullness of God.[8] (Eph. 3:14–19)

Do you *really* know that you are God's beloved? As you work your way through the ups and downs of your everyday life, how do you think God feels about you most of the time?

7. Samuel Taylor Coleridge, as quoted in *Bartlett's Familiar Quotations*, p. 530.

8. Eugene H. Peterson, *The Message: The New Testament in Contemporary English* (Colorado Springs, Colo.: NavPress, 1993), p. 405.

_____

_____

_____

_____

Do you still feel more like a slave than a friend? If so, why? What might be blocking you from opening the door of your heart to let the fullness of Christ's love in?

_____

_____

_____

_____

Satan would like to keep Jesus' death on the cross as some distant, theological fact rather than a dynamic, living, personal reality of love for our daily lives. But God is not only *with us,* as His name Immanuel testifies, He is also *for us,* giving His own life to make sure we can spend eternity close to Him (see Rom. 8:31–39).

Take some time to meditate on God's love for you as shown through His Son, Jesus. Reflect on what His friendship means, the peace it brings. Think about the images of Himself He has given in John's Gospel: the Bread of Life, the Light of the World, the Good Shepherd, for example. Write down your thoughts, so when you go through hard times that shake your belief in God's love, you can return here to regain perspective and security.

_____

_____

_____

_____

_____

_____

Chapter 3
The Promise of Persecution
John 15:18–16:4

"When Christ calls a man, he bids him come and die."[1] Those were the uncompromising words of the young German pastor Dietrich Bonhoeffer. Resolutely standing up for his faith, Bonhoeffer delivered a lecture over the Berlin airwaves in February 1933 in which he castigated the German public for craving a political idol. That idol was Adolf Hitler.

Before he could finish his broadcast, Bonhoeffer was abruptly cut off, a fateful foreshadowing of things to come. Refusing to compromise his Christian principles, Bonhoeffer resisted the pervasive influence of Nazism. That resistance led to his imprisonment in April 1943 and ultimately to his death. John W. Doberstein relates the incident.

> In the gray dawn of an April day in 1945, in the concentration camp at Flossenburg, shortly before it was liberated by the allied forces, Dietrich Bonhoeffer was executed by special order of Heinrich Himmler. . . . For innumerable Christians in Germany, on the Continent, in England, and in America, Dietrich Bonhoeffer's death has been a contemporary confirmation of Tertullian's dictum, "The blood of the martyrs is the seed of the Church."[2]

The Christian life is a road paved with the sharp stones of persecution—a truth taught and exemplified by Christ Himself, as we shall see in our study of John 15:18–16:4.

I. Persecution: General Predictions from Scripture
As we page through the New Testament, the blood of martyrs stains our fingertips. Paul's life is a good example. Acts 9:15–16 predicts the suffering he would endure for Christ, the fulfillment of which can be found in 1 Corinthians 4:9–13 and 2 Corinthians 11:23–27. And as Hebrews 11:36–38 reveals, Paul serves as a *typical* example of the Christian experience, not an exception.

> And others experienced mockings and scourgings, yes, also chains and imprisonment. They were stoned, they were sawn in two, they were tempted, they were put to death with the sword; they went about in sheepskins, in

---

1. Dietrich Bonhoeffer, *Life Together*, trans. John W. Doberstein (New York, N.Y.: Harper and Row, Publishers, 1954), p. 8.

2. Bonhoeffer, *Life Together*, p. 7.

goatskins, being destitute, afflicted, ill-treated (men of whom the world was not worthy), wandering in deserts and mountains and caves and holes in the ground.

In describing the last times, Paul peers over the centuries and issues a warning to the ones standing on the threshold of those times.

But realize this, that in the last days difficult times will come. For men will be lovers of self, lovers of money, boastful, arrogant, revilers, disobedient to parents, ungrateful, unholy, unloving, irreconcilable, malicious gossips, without self-control, brutal, haters of good, treacherous, reckless, conceited, lovers of pleasure rather than lovers of God; holding to a form of godliness, although they have denied its power; and avoid such men as these. (2 Tim. 3:1–5)

Although we don't claim it as readily as we do other Scripture verses, persecution is part and parcel to the promises of God.

But you followed my teaching, conduct, purpose, faith, patience, love, perseverance, persecutions, and sufferings, such as happened to me at Antioch, at Iconium and at Lystra; what persecutions I endured, and out of them all the Lord delivered me! And indeed, all who desire to live godly in Christ Jesus will be persecuted. (2 Tim. 3:10–12)

Yet behind the clouds of persecution brooding on the horizon, an indomitable sun shines, piercing the gloom with a triumphant ray of hope.

"These things I have spoken to you, that in Me you may have peace. In the world you have tribulation, but take courage; I have overcome the world." (John 16:33)

II. Persecution: Specific Instructions from Jesus

As we turn to John 15, we find that Jesus gives some pointed information regarding persecution.

A. Who will persecute? The sun shines brightly in verse 17 as Jesus talks to His disciples about their love for one another. Then suddenly the word *hate* is introduced in verse 18, a thought that darkens the mood in the Upper Room. The two thoughts are not unrelated, however: "The disciples must love one another because they would take Jesus' message to a world that despised them. Christians get plenty of hatred from the world; from each other we need love and support."[3] Let's listen to Jesus' sobering words.

"If the world hates you, you know that it has hated

---

3. Bruce B. Barton, Philip W. Comfort, David R. Veerman, and Neil Wilson, *John,* Life Application Bible Commentary Series (Wheaton, Ill.: Tyndale House Publishers, 1993), p. 314.

Me before it hated you. If you were of the world, the world would love its own; but because you are not of the world, but I chose you out of the world, therefore the world hates you."[4] (vv. 18–19)

The first source of persecution Jesus cites is the world, or *kosmos*. Biblically speaking, the *kosmos* is not the earth, per se, but the world system—that ravenous lion garbed in the sophisticated sheepskin of culture, religion, politics, and education. Like Hitler, the world embraces those who follow its philosophy but persecutes those, like Bonhoeffer, who resist it. In 16:2, Jesus becomes more specific in identifying the persecutors.

"They will make you outcasts from the synagogue, but an hour is coming for everyone who kills you to think that he is offering service to God."

From legalistic Pharisees to liberal pastors, persecution from the world has often emanated from the religious sector (see Matt. 23:29–35).

B. **What can be expected?** We can first expect the world to show us hate (John 15:19). Wearing many faces, this emotion ranges from indifference to indignation, from avoidance to animosity. And these faces can glare at you from your family, your classmates, your business associates, your neighbors, and yes, even religious people . . . possibly from within your own church. Verse 20 indicates we can then expect persecution.

"Remember the word that I said to you, 'A slave is not greater than his master.'[5] If they persecuted Me, they will also persecute you; if they kept My word, they will keep yours also."

There it is in black and white: the promise of persecution. The Greek term translated *persecute* means "to put to flight, to pursue." New Testament scholar A. T. Robertson says the word carries the image of "chas[ing] like a wild beast."[6] And strange as it may seem, persecuting Christians has run more rampant and ravenous during the twentieth century than it did during the first. Much of this persecution took place behind the Iron Curtain of communism, declared a leader of the underground church.

---

4. In verse 18, the syntax of the original Greek does not indicate contingency but certainty. Christians *will* be hated by the world.

5. Jesus is referring to what He told the disciples in John 13:13–17, preparing them for a life of humility and loving service.

6. A. T. Robertson, *Word Pictures in the New Testament* (Nashville, Tenn.: Broadman Press, 1932), vol. 5, p. 262.

As a member of the Underground Church who has survived and escaped, I have brought you a message, an appeal, a plea from my brethren whom I have left behind. . . . Behind the walls of the Iron Curtain the drama, bravery and martyrdom of the Early Church is happening all over again—now—and the free Church sleeps.[7]

In 16:2, quoted earlier, Jesus informs us of the last thing we can expect from the world, and that is death—"everyone who kills you." It has happened since the first century, is happening now, and will continue in greater measure as the last times draw near.

C. Why will it occur? Jesus gives us three reasons why persecution will occur.

1. **"Because you are not of the world"** (15:19). The world wants conformity. It has a certain pattern or mold that it expects everyone to fit into (see Rom. 12:2). It loves those who fit the mold and hates those who don't. And if we don't fit the mold, one of two things will happen: either we will break the mold or the mold will break us. The best example of this is Daniel, who was indicted and thrown into the lions' den because he refused to let his worldly peers pressure his principles (Dan. 6).

2. **"Because they do not know the One who sent Me"** (John 15:21; compare 16:2). Beneath its superficial surface, the world seethes in a turbulent cauldron of unbelief, resulting in resentment toward those who walk in the truth. An exemplary life rebukes everyone it comes in contact with; consequently, it stirs up a hornets' nest of emotions.

3. **"That the word may be fulfilled"** (15:25). The very existence of Christians in the world produces guilt for many people. In verses 22–24, Jesus, in effect, is saying: "If I hadn't come, the world wouldn't even be aware of its sin. But because I'm here, they're painfully aware, and that's the reason they hate Me" (see also 9:41). Remember Jesus' words to Nicodemus?

"Light is come into the world, and men loved the darkness rather than the light; for their deeds were evil. For everyone who does evil

7. Richard Wurmbrand, *Tortured for Christ* (Basingstoke, United Kingdom: Lakeland, 1983), pp. 127–28. Other books that document this persecution are *God's Smuggler* by Brother Andrew (Old Tappan, N.J.: Fleming H. Revell Co., 1968) and *Remember the Prisoners,* ed. Peter Masters (Chicago, Ill.: Moody Press, 1986).

hates the light, and does not come to the light,
lest his deeds should be exposed." (3:19–20)

Why Don't We Face More Persecution Today?

Maybe we don't experience more persecution in
our own lives because we blend in too well with the
crowd. Take Jonas Hanaway, for example. Hanaway
tried to introduce the umbrella into society when
walking the streets of England one day. But nobody
had ever seen an umbrella before. Because he stood
out so much from the crowds around him, they
pelted him with stones and dirt.

Today, an umbrella is a common possession for
most people. It is universally accepted in all social
and professional circles. But that has not always
been the case.

Maybe we've gone the way of the umbrella and
lost our uniqueness as Christians. If the verse is
true that the godly will suffer persecution, then
maybe, just maybe, our lives don't stand out enough
to attract anybody's attention . . . let alone anybody's persecution.

D. How should we react? Our reaction to persecution should be
one of acceptance, as 1 Peter 4:12 instructs.

Beloved, do not be surprised at the fiery ordeal
among you, which comes upon you for your testing,
as though some strange thing were happening to you.

Back in the Gospel of John, Jesus gives us four suggestions
on how to react, two negative and two positive, that will help
us keep our bearings when persecution starts to bewilder us.

1. Positively. First, *we should rely on the Holy Spirit.* Almost
abruptly, the Holy Spirit is reintroduced.

"When the Helper comes, whom I will send to
you from the Father, that is the Spirit of truth,
who proceeds from the Father, He will bear
witness of Me." (15:26)

Why does Jesus bring in the Holy Spirit at this juncture?
Because He is the Helper—the *paraklētos*, the "one called
alongside" to strengthen and support us. It is the Holy Spirit
who gives us our sea legs during the storms of persecution. He's the One who keeps us from falling on our faces

or getting washed overboard altogether. Second, *we should stand firm and boldly testify of our faith in Christ.* "And you will bear witness also, because you have been with Me from the beginning." (v. 27) When persecuted, rather than backing off and retreating, we need to stand firm in our faith.

2. **Negatively.** First, *we shouldn't stumble.* "These things I have spoken to you, that you may be kept from stumbling." (16:1) When we stumble, our walk is interrupted, and that is what the Lord is trying to prevent. Second, *we shouldn't forget.* We Christians are notorious for remembering what we ought to forget and forgetting what we ought to remember, aren't we? To help us break this habit, Jesus ties verse 4 around our finger:

"But these things I have spoken to you, that when their hour comes, you may remember that I told you of them. And these things I did not say to you at the beginning, because I was with you." (v. 4)

The time was coming soon when Jesus would no longer be there physically to protect His disciples from antagonism and outright attacks. By warning His men, Jesus strengthened their faith and

disarmed their disappointments. When oppression would come, they would remember that he had told them what to expect. Jesus did not want them to lose hope when the days became difficult.[8]

III. Persecution: Personal Application for Christians

As we walk away from this lesson, let's take three applications with us.

A. **There is a great difference between picking a fight and enduring persecution.** Some members in the family of God are abrasive and have an unusual penchant for rubbing people the wrong way. They start a fight; and when people hit back, they rationalize it by saying that the failure to hear truth is just another sign of the end times. Paul's words have great significance on this very point: "If possible, so far as it depends on you, be at peace with all men" (Rom. 12:18).

8. Barton, Comfort, Veerman, and Wilson, *John,* p. 316.

B. **There is a great difference between loving the world and living in the world.** It's not the Lord's plan to take us out of the world but to give us protection during the pilgrimage: "I do not ask Thee to take them out of the world, but to keep them from the evil one" (John 17:15). God doesn't want us living on the mountaintop, although He occasionally takes us there for fellowship. He wants us in the valley, where the people are. But He wants us there as pilgrims, not settlers. For the world is a battleground, not a playground.

C. **There is a great difference between running scared and being informed.** The prophetic clock is synchronized with God's time. Unhurried by wars and rumors of wars, it ticks steadily forward at its own pace, with its own schedules to keep. The Lord has seen fit to reveal some of the details, not to frighten us, but to fuel our faith (see Matt. 24).

Divine Help in the Face of Persecution

In his letters from prison, which were smuggled out by sympathetic German guards, Dietrich Bonhoeffer had these reassuring words to say about persecution—words we all can benefit from today.

> I believe that God will give us all the strength we need to help us to resist in all time of distress. But he never gives it in advance, lest we should rely on ourselves and not on him alone. A faith such as this should allay all our fears for the future.[9]

 Living Insights

Jesus has told us in John 15, "Just as the Father has loved Me, I have also loved you; abide in My love. . . . This I command you, that you love one another. . . . You are not of the world, but I chose you out of the world, therefore the world hates you" (vv. 9, 17, 19). He has not only lavished on us His love but has set us in a community of love, a refuge from a world in rebellion against Him. His actions remind us of the psalmist's words:

---

9. Dietrich Bonhoeffer, *Letters and Papers from Prison,* enlarged edition, ed. Eberhard Bethge (New York, N.Y.: Macmillan Co., 1972), p. 11.

Thou dost prepare a table before me in the presence of my enemies. (Ps. 23:5a)

Has there been a time in your life when you were pursued by enemies for Christ's name's sake? Perhaps your life wasn't threatened, but you felt the heat of harassment for being a Christian. Maybe you were rejected by your family, ostracized and demoted or fired by your employer, hounded and humiliated by your college professor. What happened in your case? How did you handle it?

_____

_____

_____

_____

_____

In the United States, we often mistake being offended for being persecuted. Movies, television shows, and art, for example, may falsely portray our Lord or deride our faith, but is this the same thing Christ is talking about in John 15:18–16:4? Why or why not?

_____

_____

_____

_____

In times when you were genuinely hated for belonging to Christ, did you find a refuge with other Christians? What difference did Christ's love for you make?

_____

_____

_____

_____

Christ wants to set before us a banquet—even in our enemies' presence—and His banner over us is love (Song of Sol. 2:4). How are you doing under that banner? Are you living in His love, obeying

His command to love your fellow Christians? Are you a refuge for others who are being persecuted?

_____

_____

_____

_____

Here's a tough question: Does your love extend to your enemies, as Christ's did with Judas? Or are you more apt to strike back or retreat? What do you need to apply in your life from Christ's model?

_____

_____

_____

_____

As you wrap up your thoughts on these issues, take Christ's words with you and let them shape not only your thinking but also your living.

"Blessed are those who have been persecuted for the sake of righteousness, for theirs is the kingdom of heaven. Blessed are you when men cast insults at you, and persecute you, and say all kinds of evil against you falsely, on account of Me. Rejoice, and be glad, for your reward in heaven is great, for so they persecuted the prophets who were before you. . . .

". . . I say to you, love your enemies, and pray for those who persecute you in order that you may be sons of your Father who is in heaven. . . .

". . . These things I have spoken to you, that in Me you may have peace. In the world you have tribulation, but take courage; I have overcome the world." (Matt. 5:10–12, 44–45a; John 16:33)

Chapter 4
Functions of the Holy Spirit
John 16:4–15

Saying good-bye is never easy, whether it's at an airport, a family reunion, or the deathbed of a loved one. The Last Supper was no exception. For Jesus and His disciples, this was their last meal together.

Like shorn sheep shivering in the chill of the evening, the disciples huddled near their shepherd that night—fearful, saddened, grieved. And Good Shepherd that He was, Jesus took them in His arms to reassure them that He wouldn't leave them as orphans (John 14:18).

Instead, Jesus assured them that His presence would be replaced with that of the Holy Spirit. The disciples understood little of what Jesus said about the Spirit that night, but within a few weeks the reality of His words would transform their lives. In this lesson, we want to discover some of the functions of the Holy Spirit—functions as active and vital today as they were in the first century.

I. Message from the Savior
On that last night with His disciples, Jesus had many things to say, including two key secrets—one about Himself, the other about themselves.

A. The secret of His victorious life. Time and again throughout the Upper Room Discourse, and actually throughout His entire ministry, Jesus referred to the vital union He had with the Father. He wanted to impress upon the disciples that the Father was *in Him* and that He was *in the Father.*

B. The secret of their victorious life. Jesus' relationship with the Father was to serve as an example to the disciples of their new relationship with the Spirit. Just as Jesus had a vital union with the Father, so the disciples were to have a vital union with the Holy Spirit. They were to draw upon the Spirit's power as Jesus had drawn upon the Father's. And just as the Father was in Jesus, so the Spirit would be in them—empowering, illuminating, directing, and comforting.

II. Ministry of the Spirit
Reading John 13–16, it's easy to see the disciples' growing panic. In chapter 13, Jesus tells them that they can't go with Him. In chapter 15, He warns of a persecution to come. Like abandoned children, the disciples suddenly feel insecure. Realizing this, Jesus explains in detail exactly how the Spirit will minister to them.

A. The reaction of the disciples. The disciples' need for support is seen in verses 4–6 of chapter 16.

"But these things I have spoken to you, that when their hour comes, you may remember that I told you of them. And these things I did not say to you at the beginning, because I was with you. But now I am going to Him who sent Me; and none of you asks Me, 'Where are You going?' But because I have said these things to you, sorrow has filled your heart."

Between the lines of these verses is a truth most of us hate to admit: we *can't* handle anything that comes along. Some things send us reeling. And we long to be held, to be cradled in security. For over three years the Lord has "held" the disciples. But now He is leaving, and they are so distraught that they're speechless (v. 5) and filled with sorrow (v. 6). The Greek term for *sorrow* means "grief," and, indeed, they grieve like bereaved children who have just been separated from their parents.

B. The solution of Christ. Moved by their insecurity, Jesus assures the disciples with these words.

"But I tell you the truth, it is to your advantage that I go away; for if I do not go away, the Helper shall not come to you; but if I go, I will send Him to you." (v. 7)

The word *advantage* means "profitable" in the original Greek. It's hard to believe that Jesus' absence could be profitable or advantageous for the disciples and for us, but it's true. Why? Commentator Edwin A. Blum provides us insight:

Without His departing (which included His death, burial, resurrection, and Ascension) there would have been no gospel. Atonement for sin was necessary for Jesus to save His people from their sins (Matt. 1:21). Also unless he departed there would have been no glorified Lord to send . . . the Counselor (the Holy Spirit) to apply the atonement.[1]

Can you imagine life without the gospel? It would be, in C. S. Lewis' words, like a world that is "always winter and never Christmas."[2] We would be stuck in our sins without any hope

---

1. Edwin A. Blum, "John," in *The Bible Knowledge Commentary,* New Testament edition, ed. John F. Walvoord and Roy B. Zuck (Colorado Springs, Colo.: Chariot Victor Publishing, 1983), p. 328.

2. C. S. Lewis, *The Lion, the Witch and the Wardrobe* (New York, N.Y.: Macmillan Publishing Co., 1950), p. 16.

of forgiveness and heaven. This is why it would be to the disciples' (and our) advantage that Jesus go away. In addition, Jesus would send a divine Helper in His place. As long as He was on the earth in His physical body, Jesus could only be in one place at one time, but the Spirit could strengthen each of them at the same time because He would work from *within.* In the innermost recesses of their hearts, where there was panic, He would bring peace. And where there was fear, He would bring fortitude.

C. **The functions of the Holy Spirit.** In verses 8–11, Jesus tells the disciples that the Spirit will have a convicting ministry in three specific areas.

> "And He, when He comes, will convict the world concerning sin, and righteousness, and judgment; concerning sin, because they do not believe in Me; and concerning righteousness, because I go to the Father, and you no longer behold Me; and concerning judgment, because the ruler of this world has been judged."

1. **"Concerning sin"** (v. 9). The Spirit, most often using the faithful, loving Christian as a visual aid (see 1 Cor. 7:12–14), shames the world and convinces it of its guilt in order to bring it to repentance.[3] Our responsibility is to love Christ and faithfully follow Him, not to bring conviction. That's the Spirit's job. What is the nature of the world's sin? Jesus said it was unbelief: "because they do not believe in Me" (v. 9b). The world is steeped in its "resistance to the light of the world, the rebellious refusal to trust in him as Savior and Lord. Sin, at its root, is a refusal of grace, the proud titanic assertion that we can atone for ourselves."[4] The Holy Spirit will continually get in the world's prideful face with the necessity of trusting in Jesus' work on the Cross to have a right standing with God.

2. **"Concerning righteousness"** (v. 10). The world's idea of righteousness is, in God's eyes, "as filthy rags" (Isa. 64:6 KJV). It allowed the Pharisees, for example, to nitpick about the Law while at the same time plot Jesus' murder. The Holy Spirit, then, will continue to do what Jesus has been doing—exposing the corruption of the world by

---

3. See D. A. Carson, *The Gospel according to John* (Grand Rapids, Mich.: William B. Eerdmans Publishing Co., 1991), p. 537.

4. Bruce Milne, *The Message of John: Here Is Your King!,* The Bible Speaks Today Series (Downers Grove, Ill.: InterVarsity Press, 1993), p. 230.

contrasting it with the light of His true righteousness. The Spirit also works through us to accomplish this (because we're Christ's chosen representatives) by steering us into a standard or lifestyle foreign to the unsaved. Since the world can no longer see the righteousness of Jesus, they can only see it reflected in us—as the moon reflects the brightness of the unseen sun. When nothing eclipses our relationship with Christ, we will reflect a true light to a world shrouded in darkness.

3. **"Concerning judgment"** (v. 11). Reading verse 11, we might assume that the future Judgment is in view. But such is not the case. The world is convicted now because a judgment has already taken place: "the ruler of this world *has been* judged" (emphasis added; see also 3:18–20). Satan stands condemned; consequently, so do those who follow in his way of life. His way of seeing things is "profoundly wrong and morally perverse,"[5] and so is the world that thinks like him. The disciples' minds are reeling by now, so Jesus saves some of what He wants to say for the Spirit to convey later.

> "I have many more things to say to you, but you cannot bear them now. But when He, the Spirit of truth, comes, He will guide you into all the truth; for He will not speak on His own initiative, but whatever He hears, He will speak; and He will disclose to you what is to come." (vv. 12–13)

In verses 8–11, Jesus revealed the functions of the Spirit in the world; but now He reveals the Holy Spirit's ministry to the believer. The first function can be seen in verse 13, where Jesus tells us that the Holy Spirit teaches us the written truth of God, which He clarifies but does not originate: "whatever He hears, He will speak."[6] Meaning what? Meaning that He speaks the thoughts that come from the depths of God's mind (see 1 Cor. 2:9–13). But this raises an important question: How can we be sure that the teaching we receive is really from God? Jesus answers that question.

5. Carson, *The Gospel according to John,* p. 538.

6. The apostles' "partial understanding of the person and work of Jesus as the Messiah would be completed as the Spirit would give them insight into the meanings of the soon-to-come Cross and the Resurrection as well as the truths about Jesus' return (cf. 1 Cor. 2:10). The New Testament books are the fulfillment of this teaching ministry of the Spirit." Blum, "John," in *The Bible Knowledge Commentary,* p. 329.

"He shall glorify Me; for He shall take of Mine,
and shall disclose it to you." (John 16:14)
The Holy Spirit glorifies the Son of God. He neither diminishes the Son's glory nor steals the spotlight for Himself. When the Holy Spirit controls an organization or a church or a life, He glorifies and exalts Jesus as Lord. In verse 15, Jesus includes a final reminder of the Holy Spirit's ministry.

"All things that the Father has are Mine; therefore I said, that He takes of Mine, and will disclose it to you."

Commentator Lesslie Newbigin sums up Jesus' teaching on the Holy Spirit for us:

The work of the Spirit does not lead past, or beyond, or away from Jesus. . . . The Spirit glorifies Jesus, taking what belongs to Jesus and making it plain to the Church. In this way the Spirit guides the Church along the missionary road whose goal is that all the nations and the whole creation should be offered to him to whom it rightfully belongs.[7]

III. Meaning to the Saint

How does all this apply to you and me? The answer lies in the two realms where the Holy Spirit works: *through* us and *to* us. First, *in convicting the world, the Spirit desires to use channels.* The Lord prefers to use living instruments as object lessons of His truth. He mentioned this earlier, in chapter 15, referring to believers as branches through which the vine produces fruit (vv. 1–5) and, in chapter 13, referring to love as the badge of belonging to Him: "By this all men will know that you are My disciples" (v. 35). Second, *in communicating the Word, the Spirit desires to see changes.* His ultimate desire is to bring us into conformity with Jesus Christ. But to stamp that image on us requires change—change in what we acknowledge as truth and change in whom we glorify.

┌─ *Let the Spirit Transform Your Life* ──────────────

In the mountains above the Los Angeles basin, towering transmission systems feed hundreds of thousands of electrical volts to Southern California. But a single home would be overwhelmed by a hundred thousand volts!

---

7. Lesslie Newbigin, *The Light Has Come: An Exposition of the Fourth Gospel* (Grand Rapids, Mich.: William B. Eerdmans Publishing Co., 1982), pp. 216–17.

33

To parcel out this electricity into usable amounts, a system of transformers breaks down the voltage to 110- and 220-volt units. This allows the residents to plug into a virtually limitless power supply.

In a sense, Jesus left to open the way for the Transformer. And the Transformer will make available to you all the limitless forces that lie in Jesus . . . in quantities you can handle . . . in just the right amount for each situation.

If you're a Christian, you have access to that power. But unless you plug into it, you'll be running your life on your own effort, your own sweat, your own steam. That's like mashing potatoes by hand when you've got an electric mixer or drying your hair with a towel when the blow dryer's within reach.

The Christian life is lived to the fullest when we're plugged in to the power of Christ.

 Living Insights

Let's augment our study of the Holy Spirit in John's Gospel by seeing what else God has revealed about Him in other parts of Scripture. Look up the following passages and write down other ways the Spirit helps us.

Mark 13:11 _____

_____

Acts 9:31 _____

_____

Romans 5:5 _____

_____

Romans 8:6 _____

_____

Romans 8:13 _____

_____

Romans 8:16; Galatians 4:6 _____

_____

Romans 8:26 _____

_____

Romans 15:13 _____

_____

1 Corinthians 2:10–13 _____

_____

1 Corinthians 6:19 _____

_____

1 Corinthians 12:7 _____

_____

2 Corinthians 1:22; 5:5; Ephesians 1:13–14 _____

_____

2 Corinthians 3:17 _____

_____

2 Corinthians 13:14 _____

_____

Galatians 5:16 _____

_____

Galatians 5:22–23 _____

_____

Galatians 6:8 _____

_____

Ephesians 3:16 _____

_____

Ephesians 4:3 _____

_____

1 Thessalonians 1:6 _____

_____

2 Thessalonians 2:13; 1 Peter 1:2 _____

_____

Titus 3:5 _____

_____

Revelation 22:17 _____

_____

How gracious of Jesus to provide His Spirit to stay with us until He returns! Take some time now to thank Him, and let the following poem shape your prayers to be transformed by the Holy Spirit of God.

Gracious Spirit, dwell with me!
I myself would gracious be;
And, with words that help and heal,
Would Thy life in mine reveal;
And, with actions bold and meek,
Would for Christ, my Saviour, speak.

Truthful Spirit, dwell with me!
I myself would truthful be;
And, with wisdom kind and clear,
Let Thy life in mine appear;
And, with actions brotherly,
Speak my Lord's sincerity.

Tender Spirit, dwell with me!
I myself would tender be;
Shut my heart up like a flower
In temptation's darksome hour;
Open it when shines the sun,
And His love by fragrance own.

Holy Spirit, dwell with me!
I myself would holy be;
Separate from sin, I would
Choose and cherish all things good,
And whatever I can be
Give to Him who gave me Thee.[8]

8. Thomas Toke Lynch, "Holy Spirit, Dwell with Me," in *Masterpieces of Religious Verse,* ed. James Dalton Morrison (New York, N.Y.: Harper and Brothers Publishers, 1948), p. 75.

Chapter 5
Four Words That Keep Us Going
John 16:16–33

The date: January 3, 1956

The place: Shell Mera, southeast of Quito, Ecuador

The hour: Early morning

Five men, whose names have become legend, sat quietly around a kitchen table praying in somber, whispered tones. Their prayers would prepare the way for face-to-face contact with the unreached, unpredictable Auca Indians deep in the interior of Ecuador. Their names: Jim Elliot, Pete Fleming, Nate Saint, Ed McCully, and Roger Youderian.

When the moment of departure arrived, the men began to sing a hymn they had come to love. Loudly and in unison the words rang out:

"We rest on thee" our shield and our defender!
Thine is the battle, thine shall be the praise;
when passing through the gates of pearly splendor,
victors we rest with thee through endless days.[1]

Minutes later, their plane was airborne. Days later, all five men were dead, their lifeless bodies found floating on the Curaray River in Auca territory.

These brave missionaries left behind a legacy. They also left behind five widows, who needed a heroism to match their husbands' to go on without them.

More than nineteen centuries earlier, another group sat around a table, only One of them knew He was destined for death. His name, too, has become legend: Jesus of Nazareth. We are told that when it was time to leave the room, those men sang a hymn as well (Matt. 26:30).

One man—John—recorded what was spoken that night. In the sixteenth chapter of his Gospel, we find Jesus' final words of preparation as He sought to brace His disciples to face life without the One they loved.

I. Confusion of the Disciples
Again and again throughout this night, Jesus has told His disciples He was going away—and they wouldn't be coming with Him on

---

1. Edith G. Cherry, "We Rest on Thee," in *Hymns for Praise and Worship* (Nappanee, Ind.: Evangel Press, 1984), no. 500.

this journey (John 13:33, 36; 14:2, 12b, 28–30; 16:5–7). In John 16:16, He tells them again, but confusion crowded their minds.

> "A little while, and you will no longer behold Me; and again a little while, and you will see Me." Some of His disciples therefore said to one another, "What is this thing He is telling us, 'A little while, and you will not behold Me; and again a little while, and you will see Me'; and, 'because I go to the Father'?" And so they were saying, "What is this that He says, 'A little while'? We do not know what He is talking about." (vv. 16–18)

Christ's main desire was to give the disciples hope, to lift their eyes from the tragedy to the glory of His impending departure. But they simply didn't understand what He was saying. So, patiently, He acknowledges their confusion and continues to encourage them.

II. Clarification from Jesus

In verses 19–33, Jesus gives the disciples reassurances that they can hang their hopes on.

A. Joy. In the Upper Room, Jesus has mentioned impending sorrow and inevitable persecution several times. Now He wants to clarify that grief won't have the last word.

> Jesus knew that they wished to question Him, and He said to them, "Are you deliberating together about this, that I said 'A little while, and you will not behold Me, and again a little while, and you will see Me'? Truly, truly, I say to you, that you will weep and lament, but the world will rejoice; you will be sorrowful, but your sorrow will be turned to joy." (vv. 19–20)

Jesus not only has His eyes on the approaching ordeal of the Crucifixion but also on the triumph of His Resurrection—and the victory over death He will secure for all who believe in Him. His disciples, however, can't quite grasp what lies ahead, and they will go through intense suffering and grief when they see their Master and Friend brutally nailed to a Roman cross and His lifeless body laid in a borrowed tomb. But, as Jesus next explains, their anguish will be like birth pangs that will give way to joy when Christ's new life is delivered into the world.

> "Whenever a woman is in travail she has sorrow, because her hour has come; but when she gives birth to the child, she remembers the anguish no more, for joy that a child has been born into the world. Therefore you too now have sorrow; but I will see you again, and your heart will rejoice, and no one takes your joy away from you." (vv. 21–22)

The joy Jesus provides is permanent—nothing and no one can take it away. Why?

Because Jesus lives forever, the disciples' joy would be endless. No one, not the persecutors, not the doubters, not the unbelievers, not the murderers, could take away their joy. This is a tremendous promise for all believers. *No one* can take away our joy! When we understand Christ's resurrection, it will have a powerful impact on our lives. The Resurrection guarantees our forgiveness and assures us that Jesus will return. Jesus' resurrection realizes our hope to be reunited with believing friends and loved ones beyond death. No opposition or criticism should ever destroy or diminish our joy![2]

As the Spirit revealed to the apostle Paul: "Neither death, nor life, nor angels, nor principalities, nor things present, nor things to come, nor powers, nor height, nor depth, nor any other created thing, shall be able to separate us from the love of God, which is in Christ Jesus our Lord" (Rom. 8:38–39). The love of our risen Lord is *always* with us—and that's cause for joy! Furthermore, Jesus promises us joy when our confusion is wiped away by clarity and we partner in His mission through answered prayer:

"And in that day you will ask Me no question. Truly, truly, I say to you, if you shall ask the Father for anything, He will give it to you in My name. Until now you have asked for nothing in My name; ask, and you will receive, that your joy may be made full." (John 16:23–24)

A Soothing Psalm for a Heavy Heart

Weeping may last for the night,
But a shout of joy comes in the morning.
(Ps. 30:5b)

B. Love. Having broached the subject of prayer, Jesus clarifies the issue of God's accessibility.

"These things I have spoken to you in figurative language; an hour is coming when I will speak no more to you in figurative language, but will tell you

---

2. Bruce B. Barton, Philip W. Comfort, David R. Veerman, and Neil Wilson, *John*, Life Application Bible Commentary Series (Wheaton, Ill.: Tyndale House Publishers, 1993), p. 330.

plainly of the Father. In that day you will ask in My
name, and I do not say to you that I will request the
Father on your behalf; for the Father Himself loves
you, because you have loved Me, and have believed
that I came forth from the Father." (vv. 25–27)
There will come a time when the disciples will have direct
access to the Father. And what will bring about this new relationship? Love. In verse 28, Jesus puts His words well within
the disciples' mental reach.

"I came forth from the Father, and have come into
the world; I am leaving the world again, and going
to the Father."

In this succinct statement, Jesus encapsulates His whole ministry. And the light begins to dawn on the disciples.

His disciples said, "Lo, now You are speaking plainly,
and are not using a figure of speech." (v. 29)

Someone up There Likes Me

Being assured of God's love does wonders to keep
us going. No matter how rough the fight, His acceptance
is like spiritual adrenaline, supplying us with reserves
of encouragement.

Do you find yourself in the ring, slugging it out with
life? Don't get discouraged. If God is in your corner, what
difference does it make how tough your opponent is?

If you're up against life's ropes right now, take a break
and towel off with these verses from Romans 8.

If God is for us, who is against us? He who
did not spare His own Son, but delivered Him
up for us all, how will He not also with Him
freely give us all things? Who will bring a
charge against God's elect? God is the one
who justifies; who is the one who condemns?
Christ Jesus is He who died, yes, rather who
was raised, who is at the right hand of God,
who also intercedes for us. Who shall separate us from the love of Christ? Shall tribulation, or distress, or persecution, or famine, or
nakedness, or peril, or sword? . . . But in all
these things we overwhelmingly conquer
through Him who loved us. (vv. 31–35, 37)

Now get back in there—and keep punching!

C. Faith. Partial knowledge characterized the disciples' lives. They grasped only a small portion of what Jesus revealed to them. However, now more than ever, their reach of faith needed to exceed what they could grasp.

> "Now we know that You know all things, and have no need for anyone to question You; by this we believe that You came from God." Jesus answered them, "Do you now believe?" (John 16:30–31)

Our faith in the Lord directly influences our growth in knowledge. The two are connected throughout Scripture. The Christian life starts with belief, and growth in Him continues in the same way: "As you therefore have received Christ Jesus the Lord, so walk in Him" (Col. 2:6). How did we receive Him? By faith. How are we to walk in Him? By faith. And, if we look closely at verse 30 of John 16—"we know that You know all things" and "we believe that You came from God"—we see a clear statement of faith even in the disciples' confusion. In the days ahead, their knowledge would come together; one by one, the pieces would begin to fall into place, and the puzzle would become clear. And what made the puzzle clear were eyes of faith—faith that the Lord not only knew all, but knew best. How about you? Do you share the disciples' faith? When you trust that the Lord knows best, your unanswered questions will be quieted.

D. Peace. If we do believe, our faith will be put to the test (James 1:2–4). For the disciples, their test was foretold in John 16:32.

> "Behold, an hour is coming, and has already come, for you to be scattered, each to his own home, and to leave Me alone; and yet I am not alone, because the Father is with Me." (see also 13:38)

But in the midst of that oncoming storm, there would be a calm, because even though His disciples would fail Him, He would still love and accept and provide for them.

> "These things I have spoken to you, that in Me you may have peace. In the world you have tribulation, but take courage; I have overcome the world." (16:33)

The source of their peace was not "in the world," but "in Me"; the strength of their courage was in the fact that "I have overcome the world." Bruce Milne illuminates Jesus' words of triumph for us.

> The last word does not lie with the evil one who draws ever nearer, nor with the tragic, rebellious world in its flight into the darkness. It lies with the Father, and hence with the one who came as the

Father's everlasting Son and Servant. Through his obedience unto death, death itself will fall defeated, and with it all the rebellious powers of darkness and sin.[3]

Jesus would not be a helpless victim but a powerful conqueror!

III. Conclusion

If we could put ourselves in the disciples' sandals, we probably would have walked very slowly toward Gethsemane that midnight hour. Our thoughts would naturally have sorted themselves into two overall impressions, probably much like the thoughts that went through the minds of those five missionary wives: Elisabeth Elliot, Olive Fleming, Marj Saint, Marilou McCully, and Barbara Youderian. First and foremost would be this: *Jesus' life may not be long, but His death is no mistake.* Following on the heels of that thought would be another: *My life may not be easy, but I can go on if accompanied by joy, love, faith, and peace.*

A Song to Light Our Way

Christ is no longer on the earth in bodily form but lives in our hearts when we accept Him as Savior. He gives us joy, love, faith, and peace—and that's what keeps us going day by day.

Day by day and with each passing moment,
Strength I find to meet my trials here;
Trusting in my Father's wise bestowment,
I've no cause for worry or for fear.
He whose heart is kind beyond all measure
Gives unto each day what He deems best—
Lovingly, its part of pain and pleasure,
Mingling toil with peace and rest.[4]

 Living Insights

How much do we really understand about joy? Let's take some time to explore this topic a little further.

In John 16:20–22, Jesus told His disciples,

---

3. Bruce Milne, *The Message of John: Here Is Your King!*, The Bible Speaks Today Series (Downers Grove, Ill.: InterVarsity Press, 1993), pp. 235–36.

4. Carolina Sandell Berg, trans. Andrew L. Skoog, "Day by Day," in *The Hymnal for Worship and Celebration* (Waco, Tex.: Word Music, 1986), no. 56.

"Truly, truly, I say to you, that you will weep and lament, but the world will rejoice; you will be sorrowful, but your sorrow will be turned to joy. Whenever a woman is in travail she has sorrow, because her hour has come; but when she gives birth to the child, she remembers the anguish no more, for joy that a child has been born into the world. Therefore you too now have sorrow; but I will see you again, and your heart will rejoice, and no one takes your joy away from you."

What do you notice about joy in this passage? For example, what will Jesus' followers have to go through before arriving at a place of joy? What will their joy be tied to?

_____

_____

_____

_____

_____

_____

How does Jesus deal with their sorrow? Does He try to encourage them to be joyful instead of being grieved? Or does He allow for the reality of their pain?

_____

_____

_____

The disciples would not take joy in seeing Jesus arrested, beaten, tortured through crucifixion, and buried. Joy would not be appropriate, would it? Often, we Christians expect ourselves and others to wear a "joyful smile" no matter what—but is that really the joy Scripture speaks of? When you are hurting or afraid, have you ever had a well-meaning Christian come up to you and tell you to smile because your gloomy face is a bad testimony for Christ? That just hurt worse, didn't it?

What does Paul tell us about joy and compassion in Romans 12:15?

_____

Yes, joy is one of the fruits of the Spirit (Gal. 5:22), but that may not mean it will be our *only* reality twenty-four hours a day. Joy will come in the morning, but before the morning there is night. For the disciples, joy would come when they saw Jesus again, victorious over death in His Resurrection.

What do we take joy in when we're going through hard times? Is it in the hard times themselves or in what the outcome will be as we put ourselves and our times in God's hands? Where will our joy come from—what is its cause? Does it sometimes come *after* Jesus has seen us through our difficult circumstances? Does it relate to a future reality that we can find comfort in now? How do the following Scriptures help you work through finding some answers?

Luke 15:10 _____

_____

John 15:10–11 _____

_____

Philippians 2:2 _____

_____

1 Thessalonians 2:19 _____

_____

Hebrews 12:2 _____

_____

James 1:2–4 _____

_____

1 Peter 1:3–9 _____

_____

3 John 4 _____

_____

Jude 24 _____

_____

Our joy is always tied to Christ . . .

- to our fellowship with Him through loving obedience,
- to our trust in Him that what He has said He will do,
- to the promise of being freed from sin and made like Him,
- to the hope of being forever with Him and all those who love Him in the place He has prepared for us.

Joy comes as a result of the new order that Jesus has ushered in through His death and Resurrection—an order that will be completely fulfilled in the future when He comes again.

As citizens of heaven who sojourn on earth, we will still have hard, hurting times, and Jesus understands this. At the same time, He gives us strength for today in the joy He has provided for eternity. And that joy can never be taken away from us, because it is forever secure in our ever-living Lord.

Chapter 6
Divine Intercession
John 17:1–19

"Take courage; I have overcome the world" (John 16:33). With this assurance of victory, Jesus spoke His last words of instruction and encouragement to His disciples. The time for the Lamb of God to be slain for the sins of the world was close at hand. It would be a time of incredible pain, a time of fear and confusion, a time of scattering. It would be a time requiring the protection of prayer, and that's just what Jesus provides now.

At this midnight hour, Jesus turns from His disciples and looks toward His Father, drawing the disciples' eyes and hearts with Him. In His prayer, Jesus would ask little for Himself but spend most of His time interceding for His men and for all the people their ministry would bring into His Father's kingdom. As Matthew Henry reflected, "When he had spoken from God to them, he turned to speak to God for them."[1]

Let's enter this quiet scene and learn what was utmost on Jesus' heart in the few hours remaining before His death.

I. An Overview of Jesus' Prayer
Scholars have called this the "High Priestly Prayer" or the "Prayer of Consecration," names that reflect Jesus' intercession for and setting apart of His disciples. In reading through these twenty-six verses, it's clear that three things were on the Lord's heart that night: His own needs (John 17:1–5), the needs of His disciples (vv. 6–19), and the needs of all future believers (vv. 20–26).

These three sections are like three concentric circles, the second of which is larger than the first, and the third of which is larger than the second, and inclusive of all three. All, however, have a common center. The prayer as a whole is keyed to one central idea, *eternal life;* for it is Jesus' petition that He may be glorified in order that eternal life may be made available to men.[2]

We'll examine the first two circles in this lesson and cover the third in the following.

1. Matthew Henry, *Commentary on the Whole Bible,* one-volume edition (Grand Rapids, Mich.: Zondervan Publishing House, Regency Reference Library, 1960), p. 1603.

2. Merrill C. Tenney, *John: The Gospel of Belief* (Grand Rapids, Mich.: William B. Eerdmans Publishing Co., 1948), p. 244.

II. Analysis of Jesus' Requests

The first circle drawn encloses only Christ.

A. Jesus praying for Himself. With His men close at hand, Jesus stops to focus His attention on the Father.

> Jesus spoke these things; and lifting up His eyes to heaven, He said, "Father, the hour has come; glorify Your Son, that the Son may glorify You." (v. 1)

Six times in this prayer Jesus tenderly addresses God as "Father." His words dripping with emotion, Jesus speaks of His impending fate with an air of finality: "the hour has come." But His death was no accidental tragedy. It was planned in the throne room of heaven, all the way down to the Judas kiss (see Luke 22:22). In keeping with that plan, Jesus asks that He be exalted by His death, that it would shine like a beacon throughout all eternity, and that His God-given authority over human souls might move from the realm of promise to the realm of fulfillment.

> "Even as You gave Him authority over all flesh, that to all whom You have given Him, He may give eternal life. And this is eternal life, that they may know You, the only true God, and Jesus Christ whom You have sent." (vv. 2–3)

Looking back on His life, Jesus reflects on His relationship with the Father. On the basis of His past obedience, Jesus now turns His eyes to the future and requests that the glory He gave to the Father be reciprocated.

> "I glorified You on the earth, having accomplished the work which You have given Me to do. Now, Father, glorify Me together with Yourself with the glory which I had with You before the world was." (vv. 4–5)

When Jesus stepped down from His throne and became a man, He not only relinquished His crown, He gave up the glory He shared with the Father (compare Phil. 2:5–8). Now, as He prepares to return to the throne, Jesus asks for His old robe back—the regal garment of glory. This request the Father was delighted to fulfill (see Ps. 110; Eph. 1:20–23; Phil. 2:9–11).

B. Jesus praying for His men. Drawing another circle to include His most intimate friends, Jesus asks several things for these eleven men.

> "I have manifested Your name to the men whom You gave Me out of the world; they were Yours, and You gave them to Me, and they have kept Your word." (v. 6)

Manifest means "to make visible, make clear." During His three years with the disciples, Jesus revealed God's "name"—that is, His character and His resources. Jesus' compassion for those in need, the serenity of His soul, the calm and quiet trust in His Father's will . . . all these qualities displayed the Father's name. The words that follow indicate that the Father truly had been made paramount in the minds of the disciples.

> "Now they have come to know that everything You have given Me is from You; for the words which You gave Me I have given to them; and they received them, and truly understood that I came forth from You, and they believed that You sent Me. I ask on their behalf; I do not ask on behalf of the world, but of those whom You have given Me; for they are Yours; and all things that are Mine are Yours, and Yours are Mine; and I have been glorified in them." (vv. 7–10)

The Father's Word, they had kept (v. 6); His provisions, they had acknowledged (v. 7); His plan, they had accepted (v. 8); His glory, they had helped contribute to (vv. 9–10). Before the Good Shepherd lays down His life for His sheep, He prays that this intimate fold—certainly to be scared in His absence—may be protected and unified.

> "And I am no longer in the world; and yet they themselves are in the world, and I come to You. Holy Father, keep them in Your name, the name which You have given Me, that they may be one even as We are. While I was with them, I was keeping them in Your name which You have given Me; and I guarded them and not one of them perished but the son of perdition, so that the Scripture would be fulfilled. But now I come to You; and these things I speak in the world so that they may have My joy made full in themselves." (vv. 11–13)

With a flock as diverse as this one, unity was no small request. These were independent, strong-willed men. Matthew—a tax-law major and accounting minor. Peter—impulsive, impertinent, and at times, impetuous. James and John—brothers who were known as the "Sons of Thunder." The character and charisma of Jesus held these disparate, sometimes volatile, elements in a state of equilibrium. But He was about to be removed from the equation and did not want this to cause the breakup of the bond between the men. Up to this point He had guarded them, but now He had to let them go.

Unity in Diversity

Jesus' overriding concern for His disciples was their unity, not their uniformity. He recognized their diversity. And He valued it.

Sometimes in our zeal to conform ourselves and others to the image of Christ, we forget that God doesn't photocopy disciples. He uses our individuality to achieve a variety of purposes—to meet different needs, to speak to different people, to fight different battles. What's important is that we're all serving the same King, united in His cause.

So, if the people around you aren't quite fitting the Sunday school mold—or even if they break the mold altogether—lighten up. God may be fashioning another Peter to turn the world upside down. Or another John to unveil the great love of God through His Son.

Jesus then asks the Father not only to keep the disciples together but to keep them from the enemy as well.

"I have given them Your word; and the world has hated them, because they are not of the world, even as I am not of the world. I do not ask You to take them out of the world, but to keep them from the evil one. They are not of the world, even as I am not of the world." (vv. 14–16)

Jesus' request in verse 15 logically follows. The enemy is always at work, so there's all the more reason to be unified. If the enemy can divide, he can conquer. There's also something in verse 15 that's easy to overlook, and that's what Jesus *didn't* ask. He didn't ask the Father to take them out of the world. He never intended them to retreat back into the saltshaker; He intended to have them sprinkled around! He never intended their lights to be put under a bushel; He intended for them to shine! True, we are not to be *of* the world. But we are to be *in* it. Philippians 2:15 strikes a good balance: we are to be "*above* reproach *in the midst* of a crooked and perverse generation, among whom you appear as lights in the world" (emphasis added). Earlier Christ prayed to "keep them" (John 17:11); now He prays to "sanctify them."

"Sanctify them in the truth; Your word is truth. As You sent Me into the world, I also have sent them into the world. For their sakes I sanctify

49

Myself, that they themselves also may be sanctified in truth." (vv. 17–19)

The word *sanctify* is often misunderstood. It doesn't mean growing a halo or glowing with spirituality. It means "to set apart for a certain purpose or for an intended use." How are we to be sanctified? By the truth. And why are we to be sanctified? To become useful. D. A. Carson elaborates.

> Jesus' followers will be "set apart" from the world, reserved for God's service, insofar as they think and live in conformity with the truth, the "word" of revelation (v. 6) supremely mediated through Christ . . . the revelation now embodied in the pages of this [Gospel]. In practical terms, no-one can be "sanctified" or set apart for the Lord's use without learning to think God's thoughts after him, without learning to live in conformity with the "word" he has graciously given. By contrast, the heart of "worldliness," of what makes the world the world (1:9), is fundamental suppression or denial of the truth, profound rejection of God's gracious "word," his self-disclosure in Christ.[3]

Being set apart from the world does not make us anti-world—just the opposite—it means that we're set aside for God's exclusive purpose, which He revealed in Christ.

> Jesus dedicates himself to the task of bringing in God's saving reign, as God's priest (*i.e.* his mediator) and prophet (*i.e.* revealer); but the purpose of this dedication is that his followers may dedicate themselves to the same saving reign, the same mission to the world.[4]

Defeat by Default

If His Word is not working in us in a life-changing way, the world *will* be. If we are not becoming conformed to the image of Christ, we will be squeezed into the mold of the world (Rom. 12:2). Make no mistake about it: dusty Bibles lead to dirty lives.

---

3. D. A. Carson, *The Gospel according to John* (Grand Rapids, Mich.: William B. Eerdmans Publishing Co., 1991), p. 566.

4. Carson, *The Gospel according to John,* p. 567.

III. Personal Applications

We can glean at least two principles from Jesus' words.

A. Genuine accomplishment is determined by God, not people. In verse 4, Jesus speaks of having glorified God by already accomplishing the work that was given Him. But He was only thirty-three. He only reached eleven men in depth. Wasn't His life a tragic waste by being cut so short? Only when seen from a limited perspective! We tend to focus on immediate results; God, on ultimate results. We see only the seed that is sown or, at best, the sprout; He sees the harvest.

B. Godly reinforcement is provided from heaven, not the world. In verses 9 and 11, Jesus appeals to the Father for unity, preservation, sanctification, and usefulness. These things don't come naturally to us. They are provided supernaturally. And they are not obtained through committee or by consensus. They are found only in Christ.

Living Insights

How often do you think of yourself as sanctified? It's probably not the first thing you think about as you roll out of bed in the morning, is it? Yet this is Jesus' prayer and His calling—for us to be set apart to spread the Good News of God's love and redemption through His Son.

This means that just as Jesus manifested God's name (character) to the world, so we are also to reveal God's character and His saving grace through our lives. That's both a great privilege and a great responsibility, isn't it? Let's take a look at the ways God has said we can reveal Him to the world.

Micah 6:8 _____

_____

Matthew 5:6–9 _____

_____

_____

Matthew 7:1–5 _____

_____

Matthew 7:12 _____

Matthew 9:13 _____

Mark 9:35; 10:42–45 _____

Luke 6:27, 32–35 _____

Luke 6:36; 10:30–37 _____

John 13:34–35 _____

Romans 12:2 _____

Romans 12:9–18 _____

Romans 12:21 _____

Romans 14:19 _____

1 Corinthians 13 _____

2 Corinthians 5:18–21 _____

_____

Galatians 5:1 _____

_____

Galatians 6:9–10 _____

_____

Ephesians 4:2 _____

_____

Ephesians 4:3 _____

_____

Ephesians 4:25 _____

_____

Ephesians 4:32 _____

_____

Believe it or not, this list doesn't even come close to exhausting the beautiful, character-revealing works God has prepared us to do through His Son (Eph. 2:10)! As you reflect on the window to God that your life is supposed to be, keep in mind the one guiding principle that sums up all the others:

Walk in a manner worthy of the God who calls you into His own kingdom and glory. (1 Thess. 2:12)

And remember why it's important for your life to point to Christ:

"There is salvation in no one else; for there is no other name under heaven that has been given among men by which we must be saved." (Acts 4:12)

Chapter 7
When Jesus Prayed for You
John 17:20–26

Sometimes, as we go about studying the Bible, we can get so caught up in what the words mean . . . what insights we can glean from them . . . what applications we can build into our lives . . . that we lose where we are. We lose what's going on. We lose who is speaking.

So right now, let's slow down.

Let's recall that Jesus is talking with His Father,
His Holy Father,
His Righteous Father.

He is centering Himself in His Father before He goes to the Cross.

He is centering His disciples—then and now—in His own heart's desire.

Let's set aside the *Thees, Thous, Thines, hasts,* and *didsts*—the "holy" language of many of our traditional Bibles—and listen afresh to Jesus' voice, hear His heart in His words. Before we take apart and study what He has to say, let's prayerfully receive as a whole the last part of His last long talk on earth with His Father.

"I'm praying not only for them
But also for those who will believe in me
Because of them and their witness about me.
The goal is for all of them to become one heart and mind—
Just as you, Father, are in me and I in you,
So they might be one heart and mind with us.
Then the world might believe that you, in fact, sent me.
The same glory you gave me, I gave them,
So they'll be as unified and together as we are—
I in them and you in me.
Then they'll be mature in this oneness,
And give the godless world evidence
That you've sent me and loved them
In the same way you've loved me.

"Father, I want those you gave me
To be with me, right where I am,
So they can see my glory, the splendor you gave me,
Having loved me
Long before there ever was a world.

54

Righteous Father, the world has never known you,
But I have known you, and these disciples know
That you sent me on this mission.
I have made your very being known to them—
Who you are and what you do—
And continue to make it known,
So that your love for me
Might be in them
Exactly as I am in them."[1] (John 17:20–26)

Now, in the still, centered quietness of Jesus' being, let's draw near to Him as we seek to understand His words.

I. The Prayer of Jesus

Let's review John 17 before we examine verses 20–26 in detail.

A. Review. In verses 1–5, Jesus prays for Himself. In verses 6–19, He prays for the eleven remaining disciples. Finally, in verses 20–26, the Lord prays for all future believers.

The Ministry of Prayer

Prayer is pivotal to the spiritual life, as spiritual men of the Bible inform us. Jesus instructed that "at all times they ought to pray and not to lose heart" (Luke 18:1). The apostle Paul emphasized the priority of prayer: "First of all, then, I urge that . . . prayers . . . be made" (1 Tim. 2:1). James, the practical exhorter of the New Testament, added: "You do not have because you do not ask" (James 4:2b). Samuel, the godly judge of Israel, declared: "Far be it from me that I should sin against the Lord by ceasing to pray for you" (1 Sam. 12:23). In his command to put on the whole armor of God, Paul instructed the Ephesians to "pray at all times in the Spirit" (Eph. 6:18).

B. Intercession. Three specific matters were on Jesus' heart regarding all His followers.

1. He prayed for our unity. In John 17:20–23, notice the three similar phrases Jesus uses to make His point:
"I do not ask on behalf of these alone, but for those also who believe in Me through their

---

1. Eugene H. Peterson, *The Message: The New Testament in Contemporary English* (Colorado Springs, Colo.: NavPress, 1993), pp. 226–27.

word; *that they may all be one;* even as You, Father, are in Me and I in You, that they also may be in Us, so that the world may believe that You sent Me. The glory which You have given Me I have given to them, *that they may be one,* just as We are one; I in them and You in Me, *that they may be perfected in unity,* so that the world may know that You sent Me, and loved them, even as You have loved Me." (emphasis added)

In asking for unity, Jesus shows that He desires "to see a deep connection between those who [are] connected to him. . . . The unity that Christ offers brings peace within and between persons."[2] So, in this request, we could say that Jesus is praying for *unity of belief* (vv. 20–21a). This unity originates from shared convictions. Belief is what binds us together. Not a vague, nebulous faith, but a very specific faith in Jesus Christ, which brings unity with the Father and the Son. The second thing Jesus prays for is *unity in glory* (v. 22). What does this mean?

Jesus gave all true believers his glory by completing his mission of revealing God (17:4–6). Jesus' work was not only to speak and model the character of God. His ultimate purpose was to present both the splendor and character of God (God's glory) in such a way that God would become personally real to the disciples. They, in turn, were to pass on what they had received to others who would also believe. Those who, in fact, received the glory would become unified by their shared relationship with Christ.[3]

If you read the passage closely, you'll discover a major purpose for this unity: that the world may *believe* that God sent Christ (v. 21) and that they may *know* this and that the Father loves us as He loved His Son (v. 23). Our unity is a public witness, an announcement to the world that Jesus came from God and that God's love rests upon us as on His own Son.

---

2. Bruce B. Barton, Philip W. Comfort, David R. Veerman, and Neil Wilson, *John,* Life Application Bible Commentary Series (Wheaton, Ill.: Tyndale House Publishers, 1993), pp. 344–45.

3. Barton and others, *John,* p. 346.

That They May Be One

When Jesus prays, it's not for uniformity—absolute similarity of organization, style, personality, and appearance. Neither does He pray for unanimity—absolute agreement of opinion within a group of people. Nor does He pray for union—absolute coalition or tight affiliation within the ranks of Christianity. What He does pray for is unity—oneness of heart, of faith, and of purpose.

Within the church of historic Christianity there have been wide divergences of opinion and ritual. Unity, however, prevails wherever there is a deep and genuine experience of Christ; for the fellowship of the new birth transcends all historical and denominational boundaries. Paul of Tarsus, Luther of Germany, Wesley of England, and Moody of America would find deep unity with each other, though they were widely separated by time, by space, by nationality, by educational background, and by ecclesiastical connections.[4]

Only through the Holy Spirit, only through faith in, and love for, Jesus can Jesus' prayer for unity become a vibrant reality.

2. **He prayed for our destiny.** In verse 24, Jesus prays:

"Father, I desire that they also, whom You have given Me, be with Me where I am, so that they may see My glory which You have given Me, for You loved Me before the foundation of the world."

In this prayer, our Lord asks the Father to secure our destiny. That security is based on the love between the Father and the Son. Can you imagine a foundation more secure? His prayer was that we be with Him in heaven, where He would be surrounded in glory.

The promise of glory is the promise, almost

---

4. Merrill C. Tenney, *John: The Gospel of Belief* (Grand Rapids, Mich.: William B. Eerdmans Publishing Co., 1948), p. 249.

incredible and only possible by the work of Christ, that some of us, that any of us who really chooses, . . . shall find approval, shall please God. To please God . . . to be a real ingredient in the divine happiness . . . to be loved by God, not merely pitied, but delighted in as an artist delights in his work or a father in a son—it seems impossible, a weight or burden of glory which our thoughts can hardly sustain. But so it is.[5]

3. He prayed for relational love. Observe carefully as Jesus calls to mind that perfect relationship between Himself and the Father.

"O righteous Father, although the world has not known You, yet I have known You; and these have known that You sent Me; and I have made Your name known to them, and will make it known, so that the love with which You loved Me may be in them, and I in them." (vv. 25–26)

The Father loves the Son, the Son loves us, and we, in turn, are to love others. This love flows deep and wide and passes over any rocks of petty differences. And, as Lesslie Newbigin notes, because Christ will continue to evidence His love through His church,

the name and the nature of God are made known. There is an area of light in the midst of darkness. There is a place where [people] can walk without wandering, and have fellowship one with another because the name and the nature of God have been revealed. That is the place where Jesus dwells and therefore where the love of God dwells. In the Old Testament the presence of the glory of the Lord in the midst of his people is associated with the tabernacle and the ark of the covenant. When John first uses the word "glory" he speaks of the word (*logos*) "tabernacling" among us. Now in the final words of the consecration prayer, he leave us with the picture of Jesus dwelling in the midst of believers as the bearer

5. C. S. Lewis, *The Weight of Glory and Other Addresses* (Grand Rapids, Mich.: William B. Eerdmans Publishing Co., 1965), p. 10.

of the love of God which the world does not know and by which the world is to be saved.[6]

II. The Application of the Message

Three specific applications emerge from verses 20–26.

A. To grow in unity means *giving in*. It means refusing to get hung up on trivial disagreements or particular philosophies. Those who enjoy Christian fellowship in its deepest sense have high tolerance levels.

B. To know your destiny means *giving up*. Being secure in our future requires that we stop striving and simply give up and trust Jesus.

C. To show His love means *giving out*. Christian love is visible and tangible. God not only tells us He loves us, He has shown it (Rom. 5:8). And we are to do the same.

Living Insights

As Jesus spent some of His last moments on earth in prayer for you, spend some moments of your life right now in prayer to Him.

With His whole prayer before you (all of John 17), slowly pray through those things that are close to His heart, bringing your heart in line with His.

Confess where you've failed to live up to His desires for unity, sanctification, love, and revealing His glory to the world. He is faithful to forgive (1 John 1:9); don't be afraid.

Praise and thank Him for His mission to save you, to bring you into eternal life, to show you His glory in heaven, to unite you with Himself, to set you apart for His holy and loving purposes. Rest for a while in His secure and encompassing love for you.

Intercede for those in the world who do not know Him. Pray for those for whom no one else may be praying. Bring the needs of your fellow Christians to Him.

Bring your own heart to Him. Ask for His help to live out His desires for you. Pray to know Him more deeply and purely.

Talk with and listen to the One who considers you His beloved.

---

6. Lesslie Newbigin, *The Light Has Come: An Exposition of the Fourth Gospel* (Grand Rapids, Mich.: William B. Eerdmans Publishing Co., 1982), p. 236.

Chapter 8
Arrest and Trial
John 18:1–24

For three and a half years, Jesus had been watched by an official band of Jewish religious leaders whose hostility grew with each passing month. With the cunning of foxes and the ruthlessness of wolves, this unholy alliance plotted Jesus' demise.

The final scenes were staged with meticulous care. An insider was contracted to help orchestrate the arrest—Judas. And with a mere thirty pieces of silver—the going price for a slave—the betrayal was sealed. At an earlier appointed time, Judas notified the officials of Jesus' whereabouts, accompanied them to the site, identified the accused with a kiss, and then got out of the way. The soldiers did the rest.

As we pick up the story in John 18, the plot has reached its climax. It is late at night; Jesus has just finished praying in the Garden of Gethsemane. It's a vulnerable, private spot, away from the city buildings that might hide Him and the crowds who might protect Him.

> But the privacy of the Passion story ended at this moment. A clanking of men and arms was starting to shatter the hush of night. Quivering daggers of orange flame began stabbing the horizon to the west, and soon a procession of torches filed into the grove.[1]

What irony. With lanterns and torches, the Roman cohort[2] searches to find the Light of the World (John 18:1–3). And the Light just stands there—without pretense, without protection—and shines openly through the darkness. But those standing in the darkness do not even recognize Him (1:5).

I. The Setting

With simple eloquence, John moves us from the quiet prayer in the Upper Room to the approaching danger in the Garden of Gethsemane, from the peace of Christ to the world's tribulation.

> When Jesus had spoken these words, He went forth with His disciples over the ravine of the Kidron, where

---

1. Paul L. Maier, *First Easter* (New York, N.Y.: Harper and Row, Publishers, 1973), p. 39.

2. The Greek word is *speira*. A cohort was the tenth part of a legion and normally comprised 600 men (though this number varied from 200 to 1,200). It was commanded by a *chiliarchos* (see v. 12). The large number of soldiers not only ensured the success of the arrest but also would have been able to stave off any riot that might ensue.

there was a garden, into which He Himself entered, and His disciples. Now Judas also, who was betraying Him, knew the place; for Jesus had often met there with His disciples. (John 18:1–2)

A. The time. It was probably past midnight when Jesus and the eleven left the Upper Room and began making their way to Gethsemane.

B. The place. En route to the Garden of Gethsemane lay the Kidron ravine, a mute portent of Christ's approaching death. A channel led from Jerusalem's temple altar to the ravine, collecting the blood of lambs slaughtered and sacrificed during Passover. When Jesus crossed the ravine, it was doubtless red with blood.[3] Still, He went forward to the familiar garden. D. A. Carson notes of this: "Having 'sanctified himself' for the sacrificial death immediately ahead, Jesus does not seek to escape his opponents by changing his habits: he goes to the place where Judas Iscariot could count on finding him."[4] And find Him he did (v. 3).

II. The Arrest

The whole garden is awash with light that spills from the lanterns and torches, revealing twelve suspicious-looking men, their shadows long and gaunt in the torchlight. Instinctively, the soldiers clutch the hilts of their swords. But they are disarmed by a soft-spoken question.

Jesus therefore, knowing all the things that were coming upon Him, went forth, and said to them, "Whom do you seek?" They answered Him, "Jesus the Nazarene." He said to them, "I am He." And Judas also who was betraying Him, was standing with them. When therefore He said to them, "I am He," they drew back, and fell to the ground. Again therefore He asked them, "Whom do you seek?" And they said, "Jesus the Nazarene." Jesus answered, "I told you that I am He; if therefore you seek Me, let these go their way," that the word might be fulfilled which He spoke, "Of those whom Thou hast given Me I lost not one." (18:4–9)

Like a lamb, silent before its shearers, Jesus offers no resistance (Isa. 53:7), which unnerves His captors. Not so with Peter. Instead, he does a little shearing of his own.

---

3. See William Barclay, *The Gospel of John,* rev. ed., The Daily Study Bible Series (Philadelphia, Pa.: Westminster Press, 1975), vol. 2, p. 221.

4. D. A. Carson, *The Gospel according to John* (Grand Rapids, Mich.: William B. Eerdmans Publishing Co., 1991), p. 577.

Simon Peter therefore having a sword, drew it, and struck the high priest's slave, and cut off his right ear; and the slave's name was Malchus. (John 18:10) Jesus responds resolutely, obeying God's plan to the full.

"Put the sword into the sheath; the cup which the Father has given Me, shall I not drink it?" (v. 11)

The snare is tripped; the prey is caught. Mission accomplished.

So the Roman cohort and the commander, and the officers of the Jews, arrested Jesus and bound Him. (v. 12)

The text states the event matter-of-factly. But the reality behind those words was brutal. A soldier would have grabbed Jesus by His right wrist and twisted His arm behind Him, forcing His hand up between His shoulder blades. While Jesus' body would have shifted upwards with His arm, the soldier would jam his heel into Jesus' right instep.[5] The brutality He would face until the end of His life was just beginning. Three things stand out in this arrest. First, Jesus had not slept that night. But even though He is fatigued, He never loses control. Second, He responds willingly. He doesn't resist, and His captors are totally unprepared for this (v. 6). In other circumstances, they had been unable to seize Him (see 7:30, 44; 10:39). But now His hour has come, and He willingly gives Himself up. The final thing we notice in the passage is His compassion, both for the disciples (18:8-9) and for His enemies (vv. 10-11). There would be no blood shed besides His. Jesus made sure of that. Even the slave's wounded ear is healed (Luke 22:51).

III. The Trials

From this point on, Jesus is no longer free. He becomes the property of the state, railroaded through the most fallacious, unfair, disorderly, illegal series of trials in the history of jurisprudence. No man was ever more innocent. No trials were ever more unjust.

A. **A survey.** In all, there are six trials—three Jewish, three Roman (the chart accompanying this lesson summarizes the trials). The charge in the Jewish trials is blasphemy; in the Roman trials, it is treason. Since the Romans preferred to retain the right to administer capital punishment, the Jews turn to their authorities, which explains why Jesus is crucified instead of stoned.

B. **Jewish regulations.** The Jews took their legal instructions from the Mosaic Law as interpreted for them in the Talmud. Judged according to this scale, the trials are weighed and found wanting:

5. See Jim Bishop, *The Day Christ Died* (New York, N.Y.: Harper and Row, Publishers, 1965), pp. 196-97.

- Arrest for a capital crime must be made in broad daylight, not at night. Verdict: law ignored.
- Arrest for a capital crime may not be made based on information by the offender's follower—for if the accused were a criminal, so were his followers. Verdict: law ignored.
- No Jewish trial may be held at night; that is, between 6 P.M. and 6 A.M. Furthermore, a trial is never to be held before only one person so that partiality or prejudice can be avoided. Verdict: laws ignored. Two of the three trials occur some time between 2 and 6 A.M., and they are before single individuals.
- Members of the Jewish court, after hearing testimony regarding the one accused of a capital crime, are not permitted to render an immediate verdict but are required instead to return to their homes for two days and nights, eating only light food, drinking only light wines, and sleeping well. Then they are to return and hear again the testimony against the accused and cast their vote. Verdict: law ignored.
- The Sanhedrin must vote one at a time, the younger men first, so as not to be influenced by the older men on the council. In the third trial, they all vote simultaneously. Verdict: law ignored.

Conclusion: this entire set of Jewish trials is a gross miscarriage of procedural law.

C. **Jewish trials.** Under Jewish law, no one person could act as a judge. The verdict was decided by a "court" of at least three. A more important case might be judged by a band of twenty-three, known as the Lesser Sanhedrin. The ultimate court was the Greater Sanhedrin, consisting of seventy to seventy-three men.

1. **Before Annas.** Notice that Jesus is tried illegally during the hours of darkness, by one man—Annas (John 18:13). Annas, the father-in-law of Caiaphas the high priest, is comparable to a Mafia boss. He is the wealthiest and most influential man of the city. He owns and operates the entire money-changing system, which is corrupt to the core and behind the group Jesus chased out of the temple. He has served as the high priest for seventeen years and is now the high priest emeritus. He is the power behind the throne in Jewry. And ever since Jesus upset his business in the temple courtyard, Annas has had a personal vendetta against Him. Gloating, the seventy-year-old Annas probes Jesus on two counts: His teaching and His disciples (v. 19). Jesus' response in verses 20–21 seems impudent, but He is merely placing the legal burden of proof

on Annas' shoulders where it rightfully belongs. A soldier rescues Annas from embarrassment by slapping Jesus down to size and putting Him in His place (v. 22).

2. Before Caiaphas. Caiaphas is the current high priest, the weak son-in-law of Annas, a pawn of Rome, equally corrupt but probably not as clever as Annas (v. 24). To grasp the full impact of the trial, let's take a look at Mark 14.

> And they led Jesus away to the high priest; and all the chief priests and the elders and the scribes gathered together. And Peter had followed Him at a distance, right into the courtyard of the high priest; and he was sitting with the officers, and warming himself at the fire. Now the chief priests and the whole Council kept trying to obtain testimony against Jesus to put Him to death; and they were not finding any. For many were giving false testimony against Him, and yet their testimony was not consistent. And some stood up and began to give false testimony against Him, saying, "We heard Him say, 'I will destroy this temple made with hands, and in three days I will build another made without hands.'" And not even in this respect was their testimony consistent. And the high priest stood up and came forward and questioned Jesus, saying, "Do You make no answer? What is it that these men are testifying against You?" But He kept silent, and made no answer. Again the high priest was questioning Him, and saying to Him, "Are You the Christ, the Son of the Blessed One?" And Jesus said, "I am; and you shall see the Son of Man sitting at the right hand of Power, and coming with the clouds of heaven." And tearing his clothes, the high priest said, "What further need do we have of witnesses? You have heard the blasphemy; how does it seem to you?" And they all condemned Him to be deserving of death. And some began to spit at Him, and to blindfold Him, and to beat Him with their fists, and to say to Him, "Prophesy!" And the officers received Him with slaps in the face. (vv. 53–65)

This is nothing more than a kangaroo court. It is illegal

because it takes place during the night, because a "preliminary hearing" isn't allowed, and because they aren't in their chamber. Not to mention the deck of false witnesses stacked against Jesus (vv. 56–59). What brings everyone to their feet in outcry against the accused is our Lord's reply to Caiaphas' interrogation in verse 61. The high priest asks Him point-blank: "Are you the Messiah?" Jesus looks him square in the eye and answers: "I am" (v. 62). He elaborates with messianic quotes from Psalm 110:1 and Daniel 7:13, and that is the straw that breaks the court's back.

Coping with Undeserved Suffering

Jesus was slandered and treated inhumanly by a religious and legal system bent on His destruction. But where others would cry "Mistrial," He demanded no appeal.

Every step of His way to the cross, Jesus left behind an example of how to bear up under suffering unjustly imposed.

For this finds favor, if for the sake of conscience toward God a man bears up under sorrows when suffering unjustly. For what credit is there if, when you sin and are harshly treated, you endure it with patience? But if when you do what is right and suffer for it you patiently endure it, this finds favor with God. For you have been called for this purpose, since Christ also suffered for you, leaving you an example for you to follow in His steps, who committed no sin, nor was any deceit found in His mouth; and while being reviled, He did not revile in return; while suffering, He uttered no threats, but kept entrusting Himself to Him who judges righteously. (1 Pet. 2:19–23)

The key to Christ's attitude was trust—not in the legal system or the religious institutions but in "Him who judges righteously."

Are you going through trials and persecutions right now? Have friends betrayed or deserted you? Are your enemies having a field day with your reputation? Are they spreading lies about you?

If so, look to the Father. He sees. He knows. He judges righteously. Someday your case will be heard in heaven, and then you will be vindicated. As for now, take comfort in the fact that He cares and loves you and will not let this injustice go on forever!

 Living Insights

The four Gospels give us the benefit of reading several eyewitness accounts of the same historical events from different perspectives.[6] Each writer focuses on different aspects, particular details, and specific conversations. As we come to the arrest and trials of Jesus, we find John's story enhanced by the viewpoints of Matthew, Mark, and Luke.

In order to gain some added insight, let's take a look at the parallel accounts of Jesus' arrest and trials. You'll find these in Matthew 26:47–27:31; Mark 14:43–15:20; and Luke 22:47–23:25. When you've finished reading, summarize the events in the space provided for you.

Summary of the Arrest and Trials of Christ

_____

_____

_____

_____

_____

_____

_____

_____

_____

_____

_____

_____

6. This Living Insight has been adapted from the original study guide on John 15–21, *Beholding Christ . . . the Lamb of God,* coauthored by Ken Gire with Living Insights by Bill Butterworth, from the Bible-teaching ministry of Charles R. Swindoll (Fullerton, Calif.: Insight for Living, 1987), p. 57.

The Trials of Jesus Christ

Trial	Officiating Authority	Scripture	Accusation	Legality	Type	Result
1	Annas, ex-high priest of the Jews (A.D. 6–15).	John 18:13–23	Trumped-up charges of irreverence to Annas.	ILLEGAL! Held at night. No specific charges. Prejudice. Violence.	Jewish and Religious	Found guilty of irreverence and rushed to Caiaphas.
2	Caiaphas, Annas' son-in-law and high priest (A.D. 18–36), and the Sanhedrin.	Matthew 26:57–68 Mark 14:53–65 John 18:24	Claiming to be the Messiah, the Son of God—blasphemy (worthy of death under Jewish law).	ILLEGAL! Held at night. False witnesses. Prejudice. Violence.	Jewish and Religious	Declared guilty of blasphemy and rushed to the Sanhedrin (Jewish supreme court).
3	The Sanhedrin—seventy ruling men of Israel (their word was needed before Jesus could be taken to Roman officials).	Mark 15:1a Luke 22:66–71	Claiming to be the Son of God—blasphemy.	ILLEGAL! Accusation switched. No witnesses. Improper voting.	Jewish and Religious	Declared guilty of blasphemy and rushed to Roman official, Pilate.
4	Pilate, governor of Judea, who was already in "hot water" with Rome (A.D. 26–36).	Matthew 27:11–14 Mark 15:1b–5 Luke 23:1–7 John 18:28–38	Treason (accusation was changed, since treason was worthy of capital punishment in Rome).	ILLEGAL! Christ was kept under arrest, although He was found innocent. No defense attorney. Violence.	Roman and Civil	Found innocent . . . but rushed to Herod Antipas; mob overruled Pilate.
5	Herod Antipas, governor of Galilee (4 B.C.–A.D. 39).	Luke 23:8–12	No accusation was made.	ILLEGAL! No grounds. Mockery in courtroom. No defense attorney. Violence.	Roman and Civil	Mistreated and mocked; returned to Pilate without decision made by Herod.
6	Pilate (second time).	Matthew 27:15–26 Mark 15:6–15 Luke 23:18–25 John 18:39–19:16	Treason, though not proven (Pilate bargained with the mob, putting Christ on a level with Barabbas, a criminal).	ILLEGAL! Without proof of guilt, Pilate allowed an innocent man to be condemned.	Roman and Civil	Found innocent, but Pilate "washed his hands" and allowed Him to be crucified.

Chapter 9

Rush to Judgment

John 18:28–19:16

Uniting against a common enemy often makes for an unusual alliance. The United States and Russia, for example, joined forces against Hitler in World War II.

Uncommon alliances also formed against Christ. One such partnership existed between the Pharisees and the Herodians.

> And the Pharisees went out and immediately began taking counsel with the Herodians against Him, as to how they might destroy Him. (Mark 3:6)

Yet these special-interest groups sat at opposite political poles.

> For while Herodians supported Rome, and everything Greek or Roman, excusing Herod's infamous immoralities, the Pharisees opposed all foreign influence and maintained a most rigorous puritanism. Yet [they] find common cause in putting Christ to death.[1]

In this chapter, we see avowed enemies join hands to annihilate Jesus. First is the coupling of Pilate and Herod, bitter enemies.

> Herod's family had once ruled Palestine for the Romans and resented the appointment of procurators in Judea. Pilate had once at least invaded Galilee to suppress revolt, treading upon Herod's toes, and suspected that Herod sent secret reports to Caesar about Jewish affairs. Yet against Jesus they are united, and that fateful day become "friends."[2]

A second unholy alliance forms between the Jews and Caesar.

> Add to these Caiaphas, declaring publicly to a Roman governor, amid Passover memories of ancient liberation, "We have no king but Caesar!" Caiaphas and Caesar, Israel and Rome—strange friendship indeed![3]

And so, in a rush to judgment, archenemies become sudden allies.

---

1. Reginald E. O. White, *Beneath the Cross of Jesus: Meditations on the Passion of Our Lord* (New Canaan, Conn.: Keats Publishing, 1975), p. 96.

2. White, *Beneath the Cross,* p. 96. See Luke 23:12.

3. White, *Beneath the Cross,* p. 96.

I. Christ before the Sanhedrin

The Sanhedrin was the supreme court of the Jews, with complete jurisdiction over all religious and theological matters. The members met in a place called the "council chamber," located in the Hall of Hewn Stone in the temple (Luke 22:66). There, and only there, could they carry out official business. And then, according to the Talmud, it had to be done during daylight hours. Luke is careful to note that the verdict against Christ was arrived at "when it was day" (22:66; see also Mark 15:1). The Sanhedrin was punctilious in its protocol. The members sat in a semicircle so that they could see one another. All charges against an alleged criminal had to be supported by the evidence of two witnesses, independently examined. When the verdict was due, the vote was taken one by one, from the youngest to the oldest, so that the younger members would not be swayed by the votes of the older members. Also, for a case where the death penalty might be evoked, the verdict could not be given on the same day as the trial. The members had to go home and give thought to their decision before returning their verdict. With the possible exception of the seating arrangement, all these procedures were ignored when the Sanhedrin tried Christ. Luke 22:66–71 is a record of the "official" meeting. In this passage, you will find no witnesses, no proven evidence, and no proper courtroom procedure. In probably the shortest of the six trials, lasting no more than twenty to thirty minutes, you will find only one thing—a rush to judgment.

II. Christ before Pilate

Because, under Roman law, the Jews were prohibited from putting someone to death, they had to send Jesus to stand trial before the governor—Pilate. But this posed a problem. The Sanhedrin accused Jesus of blasphemy. But that wouldn't hold water in the Roman court. They worshiped other gods besides Caesar. So the accusation was altered to treason. The code of law was different too. No longer was the Talmud followed; the Roman code of criminal procedure was used instead. This code involves four major steps, and all are found in the scene where Christ is brought before Pilate.

A. Step one: accusation. In John 18:28–32, the Roman trial begins.

They led Jesus therefore from Caiaphas into the Praetorium, and it was early; and they themselves did not enter into the Praetorium in order that they might not be defiled, but might eat the Passover. Pilate therefore went out to them, and said, "What accusation do you bring against this Man?" They answered and said to him, "If this Man were not an evildoer, we would not have delivered Him up to you." Pilate therefore said to them, "Take Him your-selves, and judge Him according to your law." The Jews said to him, "We are not permitted to put anyone to death," that the word of Jesus might be fulfilled, which He spoke, signifying by what kind of death He was about to die.

B. **Step two: interrogation.** In verses 33–35, Pilate begins formal questioning, probing for evidence to see if Jesus is, in fact, involved in a covert plan to overthrow the state.

Pilate therefore entered again into the Praeto-rium, and summoned Jesus, and said to Him, "Are You the King of the Jews?" Jesus answered, "Are you saying this on your own initiative, or did others tell you about Me?" Pilate answered, "I am not a Jew, am I? Your own nation and the chief priests delivered You up to me; what have You done?"

C. **Step three: defense.** Up to this point, Jesus has been either silent or evasive. Now He is given the opportunity to defend Himself.

Jesus answered, "My kingdom is not of this world. If My kingdom were of this world, then My servants would be fighting, that I might not be delivered up to the Jews; but as it is, My kingdom is not of this realm." Pilate therefore said to Him, "So You are a king?" Jesus answered, "You say correctly that I am a king. For this I have been born, and for this I have come into the world, to bear witness to the truth. Everyone who is of the truth hears My voice." Pilate said to Him, "What is truth?"[4] (vv. 36–38a)

D. **Step four: verdict.** Convinced that Jesus is not a threat to Rome and that His activities aren't treasonous, Pilate renders the verdict.

And when he had said this, he went out again to the Jews, and said to them, "I find no guilt in Him." (v. 38b)

III. Christ before Herod

Turning to Luke 23, we find that when Pilate announces his verdict, the onlooking religious rabble rises up in protest.

---

4. "In a world subject to unreality and illusion, Jesus offers the reality of a personal relationship with 'the only true God' (17:3), a life in the truth which sets free (8:32). Jesus offers that to Pilate. He, the imprisoned, offers his judge true freedom." Bruce Milne, *The Message of John: Here Is Your King!*, The Bible Speaks Today Series (Downers Grove, Ill.: InterVarsity Press, 1993), p. 267.

But they kept on insisting, saying, "He stirs up the people, teaching all over Judea, starting from Galilee, even as far as this place." (v. 5)

When Pilate hears the word *Galilee*, he suddenly realizes a way out of his dilemma.

Pilate . . . asked whether the man was a Galilean. And when he learned that He belonged to Herod's jurisdiction, he sent Him to Herod, who himself also was in Jerusalem at that time. (vv. 6–7)

Herod Antipas, the vice-tetrarch of Galilee, had beheaded John the Baptist, the forerunner of Jesus (Matt. 14:1–12). Herod has heard rumors of Jesus but has never taken Him seriously, thinking of Him more as a carnival Christ, a religious sideshow.

Now Herod was very glad when he saw Jesus; for he had wanted to see Him for a long time, because he had been hearing about Him and was hoping to see some sign performed by Him. And he questioned Him at some length; but He answered him nothing. And the chief priests and the scribes were standing there, accusing Him vehemently. And Herod with his soldiers, after treating Him with contempt and mocking Him, dressed Him in a gorgeous robe and sent Him back to Pilate. Now Herod and Pilate became friends with one another that very day; for before they had been at enmity with each other. (Luke 23:8–12)

In the face of raucous jesting and vulgar innuendos, Jesus stands in regal dignity, silent and composed. This infuriates His enemies, who wrap a kingly robe around Him in mockery and return Him to sender.

IV. Christ before Pilate

Again, a sharp rap on the door brings Pilate face-to-face with this enigmatic Jesus.

A. Playing upon sympathy. Worming out of any decisive action, Pilate walks the tightrope between upholding justice and placating the people.

And Pilate summoned the chief priests and the rulers and the people, and said to them, "You brought this man to me as one who incites the people to rebellion, and behold, having examined Him before you, I have found no guilt in this man regarding the charges which you make against Him. No, nor has Herod, for he sent Him back to us; and behold, nothing deserving death has been done by Him. I will therefore punish Him and release Him." (vv. 13–16)

71

Pilate thinks he can rough Jesus up and then release Him. But the people say no!

B. Bargaining with Barabbas. When Pilate realizes he's up against a wall, he takes another route, which Matthew traces in chapter 27, verses 15–18.

> Now at the [Passover] feast the governor was accustomed to release for the multitude any one prisoner whom they wanted. And they were holding at that time a notorious prisoner, called Barabbas. When therefore they were gathered together, Pilate said to them, "Whom do you want me to release for you? Barabbas, or Jesus who is called Christ?" For he knew that because of envy they had delivered Him up.

Pilate attempts to use a convicted criminal as a bargaining chip with this hardened crowd. Barabbas is termed a "notorious" prisoner. The Greek word—*episēmos*—means "bearing a mark"; in other words, he's a marked man, probably on the Ten Most Wanted list. The name Barabbas comes from the compound consisting of *bar*, meaning "son," and *abba*, meaning "father." Since well-known rabbis were given the title "father," it's possible that Barabbas was the rebel son of some established religious authority. Matthew tells us that this Barabbas was held as a prisoner; Mark tells us why.

> And the man named Barabbas had been imprisoned with the insurrectionists who had committed murder in the insurrection. (15:7)

Pilate gambles that this crowd, which he finds impervious to emotional appeal, will reason rationally in weighing the guilt of Barabbas against that of Jesus. But Pilate loses. The chant "Give us Barabbas!" echoes through the streets. So the murderer goes free. Stymied, Pilate tries a last-ditch effort to release Jesus, but again the crowd hems him in a corner.

> As a result of this Pilate made efforts to release Him, but the Jews cried out, saying, "If you release this Man, you are no friend of Caesar; everyone who makes himself out to be a king opposes Caesar." (John 19:12)

With these words, the crowd places on Pilate's back the political straw that brings him to his knees.

> When Pilate therefore heard these words, he brought Jesus out, and sat down on the judgment seat at a place called The Pavement, but in Hebrew, Gabbatha. (v. 13)

Matthew tells us that Pilate "took water and washed his hands in front of the multitude, saying, 'I am innocent of this Man's blood'" (27:24). Pilate knew they were shedding innocent blood. Yet no matter how stubbornly he washed, the stain of his decision would follow him to his grave—a grave that would lead him face-to-face with the One whose life he washed his hands of. In a climactic finish to the final trial, Pilate addresses the crowd.

Now it was the day of preparation for the Passover; it was about the sixth hour. And he said to the Jews, "Behold, your King!" (John 19:14)

In a crazed crescendo, the crowd announces for all eternity its verdict.

"Away with Him, away with Him, crucify Him!" Pilate said to them, "Shall I crucify your King?" The chief priests answered, "We have no king but Caesar." (v. 15)

And on the force of those words, Pilate "delivered Him to them to be crucified" (v. 16). The Scottish scholar William Barclay poignantly notes:

When the Romans had first come into Palestine, they had taken a census in order to arrange the normal taxation to which subject people were liable. And there had been the most bloody rebellion, because the Jews had insisted that God alone was their king, and to Him alone they would pay tribute. When the Jewish leaders said: "We have no king but Caesar," it . . . must have taken Pilate's breath away, and he must have looked at them in half-bewildered, half-cynical amusement. The Jews were prepared to abandon every principle they had in order to eliminate Jesus.[5]

Standing Alone

The trials are officially over. The jury has rendered its verdict. And innocent blood is fast on its way to being shed.

Pilate washes his hands.

The crowd cheers.

The disciples are nowhere to be found.

Where are you when our Lord's life and reputation hang in the balance? Do you duck down another conversational alley and hide? Do you join in with whatever

---

5. William Barclay, *The Gospel of John*, rev. ed., The Daily Study Bible Series (Philadelphia, Pa.: Westminster Press, 1975), vol. 2, p. 236.

the crowd is saying or doing? Or do you wash your hands of the whole thing, refusing to take a stand?

It's hard to stand by Christ when some are wishy-washy about Him . . . others are shouting "Crucify Him!" . . . and still others are deserting Him.

Yet, *He* will never leave *us* . . . or forsake *us*. And He will never allow anything or anyone to come between our relationship with Him.

> For I am convinced that neither death, nor life, nor angels, nor principalities, nor things present, nor things to come, nor powers, nor height, nor depth, nor any other created thing, shall be able to separate us from the love of God, which is in Christ Jesus our Lord. (Rom. 8:38–39)

Strange allies form around the cross—those standing *for* Jesus and those standing *against* Him.

Where do you stand?

Living Insights

Jesus was certainly rushed to an unjust judgment, but we don't have to rush over these events in His life. Let's take some time to slow down and walk with Him on this painful journey to the Cross.

Reread John 18:1–19:16. John's narrative of Christ's ordeal is structured around five key people: Judas, Annas, Caiaphas, Peter, and Pilate. Notice, though, that John doesn't portray one long, uninterrupted sequence. Rather, he cuts back and forth between different scenes. What do you think his purpose is in doing this? To begin formulating your answer, briefly describe the choices, actions, and emotions of these men.

Judas (18:2–5) _____

_____

Annas and Caiaphas, scene 1 (vv. 12–14; see also 11:45–53)

_____

Peter, scene 1 (18:15–18) _____

_____

Annas and Caiaphas, scene 2 (vv. 19–24) _____

Peter, scene 2 (vv. 25–27) _____

Pilate (18:28–19:16) _____

What happens to Jesus in the scenes before He reaches Pilate? What impact, emotionally and physically, do the actions of the four preceding men have on Him? (For Judas, see 13:21; in relation to Annas and Caiaphas, see 5:42; 7:21–24; 8:39–47; 17:27–28; for Peter, see 13:38; 16:32.)

In the Jewish officials' first encounter with Pilate, what issue of recurring conflict with Jesus does John highlight (18:28; see also 5:1–16; 9:13–16a; Mark 7:20–23)?

How would their role as official spokesmen for the Jews' God coupled with their behavior have impacted Pilate's ability to perceive and hunger for the truth (compare Matt. 23:13)?

How does Pilate initially respond to Jesus (see John 18:33–35, 37a, 38–39; 19:1–3, 4–5, 6b)?

What causes the dramatic shift in Pilate's attitude toward Jesus (19:7b)? What are his emotions after that (vv. 8–12)?

_____

_____

_____

What in Jesus' actions and attitude, His silent witness, would have made what the Jewish leaders claimed more plausible to Pilate?

_____

_____

_____

In your heart's eye—after Judas' betrayal, the chief priests' attacks, Peter's desertion, and Pilate's cavalier Roman brutality— what is Jesus feeling emotionally and physically at this fatal juncture before His Crucifixion?

_____

_____

_____

What are you feeling? At different times in our lives, we've probably all

turned on Jesus with anger, as Judas did,
turned against Jesus in self-righteousness, as Annas and Caiaphas did,
turned our backs on Jesus in cowardice, as Peter did,
turned away from Jesus in weakness, as Pilate did.

Jesus knows. And those who turn to Him, He is pleased to restore. That's what this whole ordeal is all about (see Rom. 5:6–11). As you close this time of study, spend a while in prayer, bringing your failures to the One who so faithfully secured your salvation. And thank Him for His steadfastness, His courage, and His great love.

Chronology of Events

In less than twenty-four hours, Jesus went from arrest to execution.

Event	Approximate Time
Prayer and agony at Gethsemane (Matthew, Mark, Luke)	1:00 A.M.
Betrayal by Judas and arrest of Jesus (Mark 14:43–46; John 18:12)	1:30 A.M.
Irregular, unauthorized inquiry at Annas' residence (John 18:13–23)	2:00 A.M.
Unofficial trial at Caiaphas' residence (Matthew 26:57–68; John 18:24)	3:30 A.M.
Formal, official trial before Sanhedrin in their chamber to confirm capital sentence (Mark 15:1; Luke 22:66–71)	6:00 A.M. ("when it was day")
First interrogation by Pilate at official residence (Matthew 27:1–2, 11–14; Luke 23:1–7; John 18:28–38)	6:30 A.M. ("when morning had come . . . and it was early")
Audience/mockery before Herod (Luke 23:8–12)	7:00 A.M.
Final judgment of Pilate (All Gospels)	7:30 A.M.
Scourging in Praetorium (All Gospels)	8:00 A.M.
Nailing of hands and feet to the cross (All Gospels)	9:00 A.M. ("it was the third hour")
Darkness (Matthew, Mark, Luke)	12:00 Noon ("when the sixth hour had come, darkness fell")
Death of Jesus (All Gospels)	3:00 P.M. ("and at the ninth hour")

Chapter 10
A Crack in the Rock
John 18:10–18, 25–27

Poor Peter. The most shameful moment of his life, denying the Lord
he vowed he'd defend, is here in the pages of Scripture for all the world
to see. But it wasn't the world's eyes that broke his faltering heart; it
was the look in Jesus' eyes that brought hot tears of grief and shame
to his own.

> Peter said, "Man, I do not know what you are talking about."
> And immediately, while he was still speaking, a cock crowed.
> And the Lord turned and looked at Peter. And Peter remem-
> bered the word of the Lord, how He had told him, "Before a
> cock crows today, you will deny Me three times." And he
> went out and wept bitterly. (Luke 22:60–62)

What was in Jesus' look? Elizabeth Barrett Browning saw both pain
and love.

> I think that look of Christ might seem to say—
> "Thou Peter! art thou then a common stone
> Which I at last must break my heart upon,
> For all God's charge to his high angels may
> Guard my foot better? Did I yesterday
> Wash *thy* feet, my beloved, that they should run
> Quick to deny me 'neath the morning sun?
> And do thy kisses, like the rest, betray?
> The cock crows coldly.—Go, and manifest
> A late contrition, but no bootless fear!
> For when thy final need is dreariest,
> Thou shalt not be denied, as I am here;
> My voice to God and angels shall attest,
> *Because I* KNOW *this man, let him be clear.*"[1]

Peter's denial is before us here in John 18, riveting our attention to
how very alone Jesus was on His way to the Cross. We will learn some
lessons from Peter's desertion, but the greatest lesson of his life is yet
to come. For in the final chapter of John's Gospel, Jesus will gently put
the broken pieces of Peter's heart back together, His grace shown to
be greater than any of our failures, His power to restore stronger than
any of our regrets.

---

1. Elizabeth Barrett Browning, "The Meaning of the Look," in *Masterpieces of Religious Verse,*
ed. James Dalton Morrison (New York, N.Y.: Harper and Brothers Publishers, 1948), p. 177.

I. Several Significant Events

Peter was known as "the rock." He was the Gibraltar among the disciples. Yet, the rock was not without its cracks. In this chapter, we'll examine the hairline fissures that led to Peter's crumbling under pressure.

A. The surname. When looking at Peter, we can't help but see his underlying potential for greatness, which Jesus saw when Peter's brother Andrew introduced them.

> He brought him to Jesus. Jesus looked at him, and said, "You are Simon the son of John; you shall be called Cephas" (which translated means Peter). (John 1:42)

Unlike what He had done with any other disciple when they first met, Jesus looked closely at Simon. Seeing inner qualities of courage, strength, and loyalty—qualities others might have overlooked—Jesus gave Simon a name that reflected what he would become: Cephas, or Peter, which means "rock or stone."[2]

B. The declaration. Peter's rocklike quality of steadfastness can be seen in John 6:66–69. At a time when people were deserting Jesus in droves, Peter stood resolutely by His side.

> As a result of this many of His disciples withdrew, and were not walking with Him anymore. Jesus said therefore to the twelve, "You do not want to go away also, do you?" Simon Peter answered Him, "Lord, to whom shall we go? You have words of eternal life. And we have believed and have come to know that You are the Holy One of God."

C. The boasting. The last time Jesus and His disciples were together, the Lord revealed that He would leave them (13:33). Peter wrestled with this and then impulsively boasted of his loyalty.

> Simon Peter said to Him, "Lord, where are You going?" Jesus answered, "Where I go, you cannot follow Me now; but you shall follow later." Peter said to Him, "Lord, why can I not follow You right now? I will lay down my life for You." (vv. 36–37)

In spite of how loyal the words appear, they are tinged with pride—a pride, as Proverbs warns, that prefaces a fall (Prov. 16:18; 18:12).

D. The prediction. The crack in the rock is detected by Christ, which leads to a prediction.

---

2. *Cephas* is our transliteration of the Aramaic word for "rock." *Peter* is from the Greek *petros*, also meaning "rock."

Jesus answered, "Will you lay down your life for
Me? Truly, truly, I say to you, a cock shall not crow,
until you deny Me three times."[3] (John 13:38)

In Mark's account, Peter is insistent: "Even if I have to die with
You, I will not deny You!" (14:31a).

II. Principles from Peter's Life

Two principles emerge from our study of Peter's life thus far.

A. No one—not even a spiritual rock—is immune to failure.
Often, in fact, the rocks are the most vulnerable. Consider
Paul's counsel in 1 Corinthians 10:12.

Therefore let him who thinks he stands take heed
lest he fall.

B. God knows our precise breaking point. Psalm 103 emphasizes that the Lord "Himself knows our frame" (v. 14a). And
He knows the stress points on that frame. He knows which
parts are subject to metal fatigue, which can be bent, which
can be broken. In Peter's case, He knew exactly when that
would occur and under what circumstances. There's a "cockcrow" in all of our lives—a definite time when we can with-
stand it no longer; and the Lord wants each of us to be aware
of our weak points so that we can brace ourselves in His
strength when that time comes.

III. Process of Denial

Turning to John 18, we'll open the door to four descending steps
that lead to the lowest point in Peter's life—his denial.

A. Reliance on the flesh when faced with opposition. Look carefully into the flickering, torch-lit garden on the night of Jesus'
arrest.

Simon Peter therefore having a sword, drew it, and
struck the high priest's slave, and cut off his right
ear; and the slave's name was Malchus. Jesus therefore said to Peter, "Put the sword into the sheath;
the cup which the Father has given Me, shall I not
drink it?" (vv. 10–11)

---

3. "According to Jewish ritual law, it was not lawful to keep cocks in the holy city, although
we cannot be sure whether that law was kept or not. Further, it is never possible to be sure
that a cock will crow. But the Romans had a certain military practice. The night was divided
into four watches—6 P.M. to 9 P.M., 9 P.M. to 12 midnight, 12 midnight to 3 A.M., and 3 A.M. to
6 A.M. After the third watch the guard was changed and to mark the changing of the guard
there was a trumpet call at 3 A.M. That trumpet call was called in Latin *gallicinium* and in Greek
alektorophōnia, which both mean *cockcrow.* It may well be that Jesus said to Peter: 'Before the
trumpet sounds the cockcrow you will deny me three times.' Everyone in Jerusalem must have
known that trumpet call at 3 A.M. When sounded through the city that night Peter remembered."
William Barclay, *The Gospel of John*, rev. ed., The Daily Study Bible Series (Philadelphia, Pa.:
Westminster Press, 1975), vol. 2, pp. 229–30.

See anything unusual? What was Peter doing with a sword? If we turn to Luke's Gospel, we'll see how this happened.

> And He said to them, "When I sent you out without purse and bag and sandals, you did not lack anything, did you?" And they said, "No, nothing." And He said to them, "But now, let him who has a purse take it along, likewise also a bag, and let him who has no sword sell his robe and buy one. For I tell you, that this which is written must be fulfilled in Me, 'And He was numbered with transgressors'; for that which refers to Me has its fulfillment." And they said, "Lord, look, here are two swords." And He said to them, "It is enough." (Luke 22:35–38)

Up until this time, which was just before Jesus' arrest, He and His disciples had been able to depend on the generosity and hospitality of His supporters. Now, however, opposition would mark their way. Jesus' instruction to buy a sword is "an extreme figure of speech used to warn them of the perilous times about to come. . . . Jesus was soon to be arrested as a criminal, in fulfillment of prophetic Scripture, and his disciples would also be in danger for being his followers."[4] Unfortunately, as so often happened throughout His ministry, Jesus' disciples took literally what He meant figuratively. So when they showed Him that they already had two swords, Jesus had to abruptly end the discussion "with a curt 'That's plenty!'"[5] Peter, then, when he saw soldiers coming to seize Jesus, fought in the flesh. But Christ's kingdom is not of this world, and neither are His weapons (see Eph. 6:10–20).

B. Reluctance to stand alone when in wrong company. Trailing the captive Christ at a distance, Peter begins to weaken. All it takes for his knees to buckle is a suspicious glance and a probing question from a young servant girl.

> And Simon Peter was following Jesus, and so was another disciple. Now that disciple was known to the high priest, and entered with Jesus into the court of the high priest, but Peter was standing at the door outside. So the other disciple, who was known to the high priest, went out and spoke to the doorkeeper, and brought in Peter. The slave-girl therefore who kept the door said to Peter, "You are

---

4. Lewis Foster, notes on Luke 22:36 and 37, in *The NIV Study Bible*, gen. ed. Kenneth L. Barker (Grand Rapids, Mich.: Zondervan Bible Publishers, 1985), p. 1583.

5. Foster, note on Luke 22:38, in *The NIV Study Bible*, p. 1583.

not also one of this man's disciples, are you?" He said, "I am not." Now the slaves and the officers were standing there, having made a charcoal fire, for it was cold and they were warming themselves; and Peter also was with them, standing and warming himself. (John 18:15–18)

Warming his hands at the same fire that warmed his Savior's captors! Hardly the place for a disciple. In fact, both Testaments give a clear warning to steer away from relationships that might cause us to compromise our convictions. As Solomon wrote,

He who walks with wise men will be wise,

But the companion of fools will suffer harm.

(Prov. 13:20)

And as Paul echoed,

Do not be deceived: "Bad company corrupts good morals." (1 Cor. 15:33)

C. Resistance to be identified with Christ when threatened by the outcome. Too often we base our decisions on expedience rather than on eternity. And we end up putting too much weight on the consequences rather than on principles. This is what Peter does as he warms himself by the Roman fire.

Now Simon Peter was standing and warming himself. They said therefore to him, "You are not also one of His disciples, are you?" He denied it, and said, "I am not." (John 18:25)

In Matthew's account, the words are even more emphatic: "I do not know the man" (26:72). If you run with the wrong crowd, it will be only a matter of time before you will have to declare your allegiance. And the pressure exerted on Peter at this weak point exposed and widened the crack in his character.

D. Rejection of the truth regardless of the consequences. Fearing recognition, Peter takes a step back from the illuminating flames of the fire. But before he can melt into the shadows, another person pulls at his mask.

One of the slaves of the high priest, being a relative of the one whose ear Peter cut off, said, "Did I not see you in the garden with Him?" (John 18:26)

Peter's Galilean accent stood out to these Romans like a Texas accent in New York City. Matthew's account picks up the discrepancy in dialect.

And a little later the bystanders came up and said to Peter, "Surely you too are one of them; for the way you talk gives you away." (Matt. 26:73)

Peter, rising to the occasion—or should we say "sinking"—lets loose a herd of stampeding expletives that kills the issue underfoot.

Then he began to curse and swear, "I do not know the man!" And immediately a cock crowed. (v. 74)

Apparently, this is proof enough for these skeptics. They know the truth that a man's "mouth speaks from that which fills his heart" (Luke 6:45b). And certainly this man's heart isn't filled with Jesus. A simple case of mistaken identity caused by the muted shadows of the dying firelight.

IV. Principles from Peter's Denial

Mingling with those shadows are two easily recognized principles that apply to us today.

A. When surrounded by wrongdoers, doing wrong comes easily. Just as it's difficult to walk through a coal mine without getting dirty, so it's difficult to be surrounded by wrongdoers without eventually doing wrong yourself.

B. The first step toward recovery is not to act like we're strong but to admit we are weak. Not one of us can condemn Peter. If we were in his shoes, we would probably have done the same. We must also remember, before we wag a critical finger, that most of the other disciples had abandoned Jesus already. Though at a distance, Peter still followed Him. True, Peter failed. But he failed in a courtyard where the others dared not set foot.

Living Insights

Oftentimes, when fellow Christians fail through their own choices, we have a tendency to want to punish them, don't we? After all, they have sullied the name of Christ. They have made it that much harder for other Christians to be respected and trusted. They have added fuel to the fire of the world's charge that the church is made up of a bunch of hypocrites.

"They knew better. They made their own choices. Let them reap what they sow," we may decide, as we wash our hands of the whole mess.

Thank the Lord, though, that He doesn't deal with us that way!

How does Jesus want us to deal with each other's faults and failures, especially when our hearts are grieved over what we've done?

Matthew 18:21–22 _____

_____

Luke 17:3b-4 _____

Romans 15:1-2 _____

Galatians 6:1-4 _____

Ephesians 4:29-32 _____

Colossians 3:12-14 _____

1 Thessalonians 5:14 _____

1 Peter 4:8 _____

Author Max Lucado has summed up Jesus' teaching in a memorable phrase: "the gospel of the second chance." Once more, this is a lesson that Peter, more than anyone else, can teach us about.

> Look in Mark, chapter 16. . . . Get your pencil ready and enjoy this jewel in the seventh verse (here it comes). . . .
>
> "But go, tell his disciples *and Peter* that he is going before you to Galilee." . . .
>
> What a line. It's as if all of heaven had watched Peter fall—and it's as if all of heaven wanted to help him back up again. "Be sure and tell Peter that he's not left out. Tell him that one failure doesn't make a flop." . . .
>
> Those who know these types of things say that the Gospel of Mark is really the transcribed notes and dictated thoughts of Peter. If this is true, then it was Peter himself who included these two words! And if these really are his words, I can't help but imagine that the old fisherman had to brush away a tear and swallow a lump when he got to this point in the story. . . .
>
> It's not every day that you find someone who will give you a second chance—much less someone who will give you a second chance every day.
>
> But in Jesus, Peter found both.[6]

6. Max Lucado, *No Wonder They Call Him the Savior* (Portland, Ore.: Multnomah Press, 1986), pp. 93–95.

Chapter 11

Death on a Cross

John 19:16–37

A cross hung around your neck or pinned to your lapel tells the world of your faith. It also symbolizes a certain morality adhered to by Christians. And wearing it often brings a degree of respect from others.

But take that tiny piece of jewelry back in time two thousand years and try wearing it around your neck or on your toga. People would give you puzzled, suspicious looks, thinking you were some kind of lunatic.

For back then, the cross was not a symbol of faith but of failure, not of morality but of lawlessness, not of respect but of unspeakable shame.

Then, the cross was not polished and esteemed. It loomed menacingly on the frayed hem of the city's outskirts, overlooking the garbage dumps. Made of rough-cut timbers and iron spikes, it stood ominously on the horizon . . . a sentry at attention, standing watch for any enemies of the empire . . . a stoic monument that crimes against the state do not pay . . . a splintered vestige of barbarism in the architecture of a renowned civilization.

For Jesus—who had no room in the inn at His birth and "nowhere to lay His head" during His life (Matt. 8:20)—the cross was a final place of rest. There He raised His weary, bloodstained head and asked the Judge of the universe not for vengeance, or even for justice, but for mercy on those who crucified and cursed Him. There humanity received a second chance. And an eagerly awaiting Father received His Son.

That is why, for two thousand years, the cross has captured the attention of artists, poets, architects, and yes, even jewelers. In the cruel brutality, they each see something beautiful; in the rough-cut wood, something golden.

I. Introductory Information

Before we look at our passage in John, it will help to get a biblical and historical orientation to Jesus' Crucifixion.

A. Scriptural predictions. Some people have the false impression that Jesus was a helpless victim of an insidious plot, a pitiful martyr whose plans were suddenly and unexpectedly terminated by a cross. Such was not the case at all. His Crucifixion had been carefully predicted in the Scriptures.

1. In the Old Testament. Written centuries before Christ, several passages in the Old Testament clearly prophesy the Messiah's Crucifixion. One of the most prominent is

Psalm 22, which tells of hands and feet that are pierced (v. 16b), of bones pulled out of joint (vv. 14, 17), of clothing divided (v. 18), and of scorning and mocking (vv. 7, 12–13, 17b). Another prophetic text is Isaiah 53. It describes the misery, torture, and pain of God's Servant (vv. 3, 5, 7, 11), the Lord God's planning of the Servant's death (v. 10), and His being crucified with sinners (v. 12).

    2. In the New Testament. Acts 2:23 explicitly states that Jesus was "delivered up by the predetermined plan and foreknowledge of God." In Acts 3:18, Peter informs us that this predetermined plan was "announced beforehand by the mouth of all the prophets." The evidence is abundant and clear: Jesus was not murdered by an abrupt act of passion; His death was planned by God.

  B. Historical orientation. The temporal and geographical information leading up to the Crucifixion will serve to paint the historical backdrop.

    1. The time. After Pilate's verdict, the governor delivered Jesus over to be crucified (John 19:16; Mark 15:15). This probably occurred between 7:30 and 8:00 in the morning.

    2. The place. The actual sentencing of Jesus took place at the judgment hall located near Herod's temple. John's account helps us pinpoint the exact place.

> When Pilate therefore heard these words, he brought Jesus out, and sat down on the judgment seat at a place called The Pavement, but in Hebrew, Gabbatha. (John 19:13)

Recent excavations have uncovered what may be the site —a large, elevated, paved area at the northwest corner of the temple site that was part of the Castle Antonia. Roman soldiers stayed in this castle during Passover to maintain law and order. Doubtless, they looked down from their windows as Pilate presented Jesus to the people. For them, this was great sport.

II. Christ's Suffering

Step by agonizing step, we'll walk with Jesus through that momentous last day of His earthly life.

  A. Scourging of the victim. Although it was unwarranted and unnecessary, Pilate had Jesus scourged (Matt. 27:26; Mark 15:15). There were two kinds of scourging in Jesus' day, Jewish and Roman. Jewish law specified that the victim could not receive more than forty lashes (Deut. 25:1–3). Roman law was not so humane. A man trained in torture, called a lictor, administered the scourging.

He used a short circular piece of wood, to which were attached several strips of leather. At the end of each strip, he sewed a chunk of bone or a small piece of iron chain. This instrument was called a flagellum. There was no set number of stripes to be administered, and the law said nothing about the parts of the body to be assailed.[1]

Jesus was stripped and then tied to a low stone column. In vivid detail, modern-day medical doctors recreate the gruesome event.

As the Roman soldiers repeatedly struck the victim's back with full force, the iron balls would cause deep contusions, and the leather thongs and sheep bones would cut into the skin and subcutaneous tissues. Then, as the flogging continued, the lacerations would tear into the underlying skeletal muscles and produce quivering ribbons of bleeding flesh. Pain and blood loss generally set the stage for circulatory shock. The extent of blood loss may well have determined how long the victim would survive on the cross. . . .

The severe scourging, with its intense pain and appreciable blood loss, most probably left Jesus in a preshock state. Moreover, hematidrosis had rendered his skin particularly tender. The physical and mental abuse meted out by the Jews and the Romans, as well as the lack of food, water, and sleep, also contributed to his generally weakened state. Therefore, even before the actual crucifixion, Jesus' physical condition was at least serious and possibly critical.[2]

B. Mocking by the soldiers. But the suffering would not end here. Cruel soldiers, who have circled around Christ's bloody body like vultures, move in to pick at the remains.

Then the soldiers of the governor took Jesus into the Praetorium and gathered the whole Roman cohort around Him. And they stripped Him, and put a scarlet robe on Him. And after weaving a crown of thorns, they put it on His head, and a reed in His

---

1. Jim Bishop, *The Day Christ Died* (New York, N.Y.: Harper and Brothers, 1957), pp. 290–91.

2. William D. Edwards, M.D., Wesley J. Gabel, M.Div., and Floyd E. Hosmer, M.S., A.M.I., "On the Physical Death of Jesus Christ," in *JAMA: The Journal of the American Medical Association*, March 21, 1986, pp. 1457–58.

right hand; and they kneeled down before Him and mocked Him, saying, "Hail, King of the Jews!" And they spat on Him, and took the reed and began to beat Him on the head. And after they had mocked Him, they took His robe off and put His garments on Him, and led Him away to crucify Him. (Matt. 27:27–31)

In raucous sport, they place a robe on Jesus. But not a long, flowing robe. The Greek term used is *chlamus*, a short cloak worn over the shoulders. Standing there, naked from the waist down, Jesus becomes the object of their vulgar remarks. Each tries to top the other's joke. Each takes his turn, spitting on Him . . . cursing His name . . . slapping Him with the reed . . . punching His raw chest with their fists. Him, upon whom God would soon bestow a name that was above every other. Him, at whose name every knee would someday bow, of those who are in heaven, and on the earth, and under the earth. Him, before whom every tongue would someday confess that He is Lord (Phil. 2:9–11). But for now, humanity offers this King only spit . . . expletives . . . and fists.

C. Walking to the site. Criminals were commonly paraded through town, and no exception was made in Jesus' case (Matt. 27:31; John 19:17a). Generally, the victim was surrounded by four Roman soldiers, led by a centurion, and was made to carry the six-foot crossbeam that would later be attached to the larger, vertical post of the cross. After the beating and scourging, however, Jesus was too weak to carry His cross all the way to Golgotha, the Place of a Skull, so Simon of Cyrene was pressed into service to help Him (v. 17; Matt. 27:32). Above His head hung a 12- by 24-inch placard declaring His crime: "JESUS THE NAZARENE, THE KING OF THE JEWS" (John 19:19). Pilate had this message written in Hebrew, Latin, and Greek so no one would miss the meaning of what was about to happen (v. 20). But the chief priests, notorious for straining at gnats while overlooking the important things, objected to the wording.

And so the chief priests of the Jews were saying to Pilate, "Do not write, 'The King of the Jews'; but that He said, 'I am King of the Jews.'" Pilate answered, "What I have written I have written." (vv. 21–22)

D. Nailing on the cross. Crucifixion was a barbaric form of capital punishment that began in Persia. The Persians believed that the earth was sacred to Ormuzd, the earth god, so death should not contaminate the earth. Therefore, criminals were fastened to vertical shafts of wood by iron spikes and suspended above the earth . . . to die from exposure, exhaustion, or suffocation. Death was painfully slow and publicly humiliating. Jim Bishop again conveys the horror.

> The executioner laid the crossbeam behind Jesus and brought him to the ground quickly by grasping his arm and pulling him backward. As soon as Jesus fell, the beam was fitted under the back of his neck and, on each side, soldiers quickly knelt on the inside of the elbows. . . . The thorns pressed against his torn scalp.
>
> . . . With his right hand, the executioner probed the wrist of Jesus to find the little hollow spot. When he found it, he took one of the square-cut iron nails . . . raised the hammer over the nail head and brought it down with force. . . .
>
> Two soldiers grabbed each side of the crossbeam and lifted. As they pulled up, they dragged Jesus by the wrists. With every breath, he groaned. When the soldiers reached the upright, the four of them began to lift the crossbeam higher until the feet of Jesus were off the ground. The body must have writhed with pain. . . .
>
> When the crossbeam was set firmly, the executioner . . . knelt before the cross. Two soldiers hurried to help, and each one took hold of a leg at the calf. The ritual was to nail the right foot over the left, and this was probably the most difficult part of the work. If the feet were pulled downward, and nailed close to the foot of the cross, the prisoner always died quickly. Over the years, the Romans learned to push the feet upward on the cross, so that the condemned man could lean on the nails and stretch himself upward [to breathe].[3]

Helplessly suspended between heaven and earth, Jesus could look down and see the soldiers gambling for His clothes, unknowingly playing their part in the fulfillment of Scripture (John 19:23–24). More painful, though, was the reflected agony in His mother's eyes—she and her sister, as well as Mary the wife of Clopas and Mary Magdalene, were huddled together trying to endure this unendurable ordeal. And there was John,

3. Bishop, *The Day Christ Died*, pp. 311–12.

the disciple whom Jesus loved. Seeing His friend, Jesus managed to gasp out to His mother, "Woman, behold, your son!" And to John, "Behold, your mother!" Even to the last, Jesus took care of those He loved, and John took Mary into his home "from that hour" (vv. 25–27).

E. **Dying from the pain.** Excruciating pain accompanied every upward push for breath and every downward release from fatigue. Each movement cut deeper into bone and tendons and raw muscle. Fever inevitably set in, inflaming the wounds and creating an insatiable thirst. Waves of hallucinations drifted the victim in and out of consciousness. And in time, flies and other insects found their way to the open wounds. At this point, Jesus knew that He had accomplished everything the Father had sent Him to do. To fulfill one last Scripture (see Ps. 69:3, 21), He said,

> "I am thirsty." A jar full of sour wine was standing there; so they put a sponge full of the sour wine upon a branch of hyssop, and brought it up to His mouth. When Jesus therefore had received the sour wine, He said, "It is finished!" And He bowed His head, and gave up His spirit. (John 19:28b–30)

With a loud shout, *"Tetelestai"*—"It is finished!"—Jesus died with an exclamation "of triumph on his lips. He did not say, 'It is finished,' in weary defeat; he said it as one who shouts for joy. . . . He seemed to be broken on the Cross, but he knew that his victory was won."[4]

F. **Dealing with the body.** John, the only disciple at the foot of the cross, gives us an eyewitness account of what was done with Jesus' body.

> The Jews therefore, because it was the day of preparation, so that the bodies should not remain on the cross on the Sabbath (for that Sabbath was a high day), asked Pilate that their legs might be broken, and that they might be taken away. The soldiers therefore came, and broke the legs of the first man, and of the other man who was crucified with Him; but coming to Jesus, when they saw that He was already dead, they did not break His legs; but one of the soldiers pierced His side with a spear, and immediately there came out blood and water. And he who has seen has borne witness, and his

4. William Barclay, *The Gospel of John,* rev. ed., The Daily Study Bible Series (Philadelphia, Pa.: Westminster Press, 1975), vol. 2, p. 258.

witness is true; and he knows that he is telling the truth, so that you also may believe. For these things came to pass, that the Scripture might be fulfilled, "Not a bone of Him shall be broken." And again another Scripture says, "They shall look on Him whom they pierced." (vv. 31–37)

To speed up death, soldiers would break the victims' legs so they could no longer raise themselves to inhale. But with Jesus, that wasn't necessary. To make sure He hadn't simply passed out, a soldier thrust a spear into Jesus' side.[5]

Make the Cross Your Focal Point

Take a few minutes now to fix your eyes upon Jesus, the author and perfecter of our faith,
> who for the joy set before Him endured the cross, despising the shame, and has sat down at the right hand of the throne of God. For consider Him who has endured such hostility by sinners against Himself, so that you may not grow weary and lose heart. (Heb. 12:2–3)

Now look more intently. Squint your eyes into the darkness of that brutal day. See *how* He suffered. Peter, who was standing in the distant shadows, strained his eyes. And this is what he saw.
> And while being reviled, He did not revile in return; while suffering, He uttered no threats, but kept entrusting Himself to Him who judges righteously. (1 Pet. 2:23)

It's hard to look at the shame and suffering Christ endured on the cross. But if we will, our perspective on our own circumstances will never be the same.

If you're weary and losing heart, take a rest. And while you catch your breath, look up the hill . . . up to the One who went before you . . . the One who pioneered the trail so you could follow in His steps (2:21).

---

5. One sign of death is the quick separation of dark red corpuscles from the thin, whitish serum of the blood, here called "water" (v. 34). Normally, the dead do not bleed. But after death, the right auricle of the human heart fills with blood, and the membrane surrounding the heart, the pericardium, holds the watery serum. Jesus' heart must have been punctured with the spear, causing both fluids to flow from His side.

Living Insights

"It is finished!" With these words, the Good Shepherd lays down His life for His sheep . . . the Light of the World closes His eyes and pillows His head on His Father's chest. And He rests from His work.

What indescribable love hangs on a cross and dies to bring sinful human beings to heaven!

Thoughtfully and prayerfully, read the following passages and see a few of the things Christ has accomplished for you.

Romans 3:22–26 _____

_____

_____

2 Corinthians 5:17–21 _____

_____

_____

Ephesians 1:7 _____

_____

_____

Colossians 1:19–22 _____

_____

_____

1 Peter 1:3–4 _____

_____

_____

1 John 5:11 _____

_____

_____

Yes, it is finished. The sinless One took on our sins, paid for our crimes, hung in our place. He died that we might live. Spend some time in prayer, thanking Him, asking Him to let this reality sink more deeply into your heart, telling Him how much you love Him. There was no other way to heaven but through the ordeal of the Cross. Remember that. And remember the One who considered it a victory for you.

The Choice of the Cross

Hard it is, very hard,
To travel up the slow and stony road
To Calvary, to redeem mankind; far better
To make but one resplendent miracle,
Lean through the cloud, lift the right hand of power
And with a sudden lightning smite the world perfect.
Yet this was not God's way, Who had the power,
But set it by, choosing the cross, the thorn,
The sorrowful wounds. Something there is, perhaps,
That power destroys in passing, something supreme,
To whose great value in the eyes of God
That cross, that thorn, and those five wounds bear witness.[6]

6. Dorothy L. Sayers, "The Choice of the Cross," in *Masterpieces of Religious Verse,* ed. James Dalton Morrison (New York, N.Y.: Harper and Brothers Publishers, 1948), p. 189.

Chapter 12

A Miraculous Resurrection

John 19:38–20:10

"It is finished." To John, this must have sounded more like, "It's all over." Jesus' bloody body finally sagged on the cross, finally still, finally quiet.

The One who had snatched the official's son back from death and called Lazarus out of his tomb—the Resurrection and the Life—now hung limp and lifeless, needing to be placed in a tomb Himself.

John remembered Jesus' words:

"For just as the Father raises the dead and gives them life, even so the Son also gives life to whom He wishes." (John 5:21)

"I am the bread of life. . . . If anyone eats of this bread, he shall live forever." (6:48, 51b)

"I am the light of the world; he who follows Me shall not walk in the darkness, but shall have the light of life." (8:12)

"I am the good shepherd . . . and I lay down My life for the sheep . . . that I may take it again. No one has taken it away from Me, but I lay it down on My own initiative. I have authority to lay it down, and I have authority to take it up again." (10:14, 15b, 17b–18a)

"I am the resurrection and the life; he who believes in Me shall live even if he dies, and everyone who lives and believes in Me shall never die." (11:25–26a)

"Truly, truly, I say to you, that you will weep and lament, but the world will rejoice; you will be sorrowful, but your sorrow will be turned to joy. . . . I will see you again, and your heart will rejoice." (16:20, 22a)

"These things I have spoken to you, that in Me you may have peace. In the world you have tribulation, but take courage; I have overcome the world." (v. 33)

Was it all just a dream? John must have wondered. *What did these past three years mean? The healings, the signs, the profound teaching— how could it all end like this? How are joy and peace possible now?*

This chapter has been adapted from the study guide *The Majesty of God's Son,* from the Bible-teaching ministry of Charles R. Swindoll (Anaheim, Calif.: Insight for Living, 1999), pp. 127–35.

Jesus was dead. *Jesus was dead!* As John watched Joseph of Arimathea and Nicodemus take His battered body off the cross, confusion and despair flooded his soul.

Yes, it was "finished"; but, as John would soon see, it was far from over.

I. The Certainty of His Death

Later, people would say Jesus couldn't really have been dead. He must have been unconscious or in a coma and later came to in the tomb. But the separation of the blood and water in His body (John 19:34–35) made that medically impossible. Even the soldiers knew He was really dead (vv. 32–33). More certainly than that, though, His friends knew.

> And after these things Joseph of Arimathea, being a disciple of Jesus, but a secret one, for fear of the Jews, asked Pilate that he might take away the body of Jesus; and Pilate granted permission. He came therefore, and took away His body. And Nicodemus came also, who had first come to Him by night; bringing a mixture of myrrh and aloes, about a hundred pounds weight. And so they took the body of Jesus, and bound it in linen wrappings with the spices, as is the burial custom of the Jews. (vv. 38–40)

Today, we leave the care of the dead to the undertaker, grateful for clean, quiet viewing rooms, flowers, and funereal dignity. In Jesus' time, however, family and friends were responsible for preparing the body for burial. The custom of the Jews was to wrap the entire body in strips of cloth, sprinkling a mixture of pulverized myrrh and aloe between the layers to glue them together and stifle the smell of death's decay. Joseph and Nicodemus were friends of Jesus. Had there been the faintest pulse of life in His limp body, wouldn't they have made every effort to resuscitate Him? Of course. But they prepared Him for burial according to Jewish custom.

II. The Finality of the Tomb

Jesus' body was then entombed.

> Now in the place where He was crucified there was a garden; and in the garden a new tomb in which no one had yet been laid. Therefore on account of the Jewish day of preparation, because the tomb was nearby, they laid Jesus there. (vv. 41–42)

"The Jewish day of preparation" refers to the Sabbath, which began at sundown on Friday. This makeshift mortuary crew had only a short time in which to accomplish their task. To save time, Joseph of Arimathea volunteered his own tomb, a newly hewn cave of rock. Even in death, however, Jesus' prisoner status continued. In addition to the huge stone that sealed the tomb (Matt. 27:60), Pilate gave in to pressure from the Jewish leaders and ordered a guard to keep watch outside (vv. 62–66). The chief priests and Pharisees even set a seal on the stone, which consisted of a cord stretched across the stone and fastened at each end by sealing wax or clay.[1] Anyone who broke that seal, which was official,[2] would incur the wrath of the Roman government.

III. The Reality of His Resurrection

For the people who loved Jesus, who had abandoned everything to follow Him, the darkness of that first Easter morning three days later must have seemed a metaphor for their lives. The women came first.

> Now on the first day of the week Mary Magdalene came early to the tomb, while it was still dark. (John 20:1a)

According to Mark and Luke (Mark 16:1; Luke 24:1, 10), Mary the mother of James, Joanna, and Salome, along with a few other unnamed women, accompanied Mary Magdalene that morning. Having waited through what was surely an interminable Sabbath day, the women crept through the quiet predawn darkness toward the tomb, carrying the spices with which they hoped to anoint the body (Luke 24:1).[3] No doubt their nerves were already on edge. They were, after all, in a cemetery, just days after witnessing the most horrific death imaginable. And an earthquake had just further jolted their world (see Matt. 28:2).[4] As if that weren't enough, the sight they came upon must have shaken them to the core.

> The stone [was] already taken away from the tomb. (John 20:1b)

1. Robert H. Mounce, *Matthew,* Good News Commentary series (San Francisco, Calif.: Harper and Row, Publishers, 1985), p. 271.

2. D. A. Carson, "Matthew," in *The Expositor's Bible Commentary,* gen. ed. Frank E. Gaebelein (Grand Rapids, Mich.: Zondervan Publishing House, Regency Reference Library, 1984), vol. 8, p. 586.

3. Jesus' body had already been anointed by Joseph of Arimathea and Nicodemus (John 19:38–40). So why are the women coming to anoint Him a second time? Leon Morris tells us that "presumably this means that the burial on the Friday had had to be hurried, and when the Sabbath was over the ladies wished to complete the burial in a seemly manner." *The Gospel according to John,* rev. ed., The New International Commentary on the New Testament Series (Grand Rapids, Mich.: William B. Eerdmans Publishing Co., 1995), p. 732.

4. *The Narrated Bible: In Chronological Order* harmonizes or combines the Gospel accounts to give this order of events for that resurrection morning: (1) the earthquake from the angel who rolled back the stone, (2) the women bring spices to anoint Jesus' body and wonder who will roll away the stone, (3) they find the stone has been rolled away, (4) the angel announces that Jesus is risen and tells the women to tell His disciples, (5) two more angels remind the women of Christ's prophecy about His rising, (6) Mary Magdalene tells Peter and John the amazing news. Narration by F. LaGard Smith (Eugene, Ore.: Harvest House Publishers, 1984), p. 1478.

These women had watched Nicodemus and Joseph of Arimathea roll that stone into place. They had heaved it onto its edge and maneuvered it into an inclined groove, then wedged it into place with some wood or a rock. Once Jesus' body was inside the tomb, they removed the wedge and the stone rolled into place. It was not uncommon for such a stone to weigh a ton. Who, then, could— or would—have moved it? Not the guards; they would have feared punishment. And the disciples couldn't have because of the presence of the guards. Mary Magdalene and the other women didn't know what happened, and they were frantic.

> So she ran and came to Simon Peter, and to the other disciple whom Jesus loved, and said to them, "They have taken away the Lord out of the tomb, and we do not know where they have laid Him." (v. 2)

Though Mary didn't understand, it was Easter Sunday morning, and the sun had finally risen. Peter and John wasted no time in running toward the light.

> Peter therefore went forth, and the other disciple, and they were going to the tomb. And the two were running together; and the other disciple ran ahead faster than Peter, and came to the tomb first; and stooping and looking in, he *saw* the linen wrappings lying there; but he did not go in. (vv. 3–5, emphasis added)

Notice the word *saw*. John uses three different Greek words for it in verses 3–9, each marking a progression from physical to spiritual sight. Here in verse 5, the Greek word for *saw* is *blepei*.[5] It basically means "to note," with a strong "emphasis on the function of the eye."[6] John peered into the cave and noticed the linen wrappings, but their significance did not immediately hit him.

> Simon Peter therefore also came, following him, and entered the tomb; and he *beheld* the linen wrappings lying there, and the face-cloth, which had been on His head, not lying with the linen wrappings, but rolled up in a place by itself. (vv. 6–7, emphasis added)

Next came Simon Peter, puffing up behind John. Shouldering past John into the tomb, he "beheld" what John had seen but in a

5. Edwin A. Blum, "John," in *The Bible Knowledge Commentary*, New Testament edition, ed. John F. Walvoord and Roy B. Zuck (Colorado Springs, Colo.: Chariot Victor Publishing, 1983), p. 342.

6. Gerhard Kittel and Gerhard Friedrich, eds., *Theological Dictionary of the New Testament*, translated and abridged in one volume by Geoffrey W. Bromiley (1985; reprint, Grand Rapids, Mich.: William B. Eerdmans Publishing Co., 1992), p. 706.

different way. The Greek word this time is *theōrei*,[7] from which we get our word *theorize*. Peter saw something he wasn't expecting, and it stopped him in his tracks. Eyes narrowed, brow furrowed, he studied it and pondered what it could mean. Merrill Tenney offers some insight into what it was that so arrested Peter's attention.

> Why should the condition of the graveclothes excite Peter's amazement? . . .
> There is a strong hint that the clothes were not folded as if Jesus had unwound them and then deposited them in two neat piles on the shelf. The word used to describe the napkin or head cloth does not connote a flat folded square like a table napkin, but a ball of cloth bearing the appearance of being rolled around an object that was no longer there. The wrappings were in position where the body had lain, and the head cloth was where the head had been, separated from the others by the distance from armpits to neck. The shape of the body was still apparent in them, but the flesh and bone had disappeared.[8]

Empty graveclothes—but their shape intact, like the shell of a locust still clinging to a tree or an opened cocoon still dangling from a leaf. Tenney adds, "The tomb had not been opened to let Jesus out, but to let in the disciples. Transformed by the resurrection, He had passed through the grave clothes, leaving like an outworn chrysalis the cerements of the tomb for the vestments of glory."[9] Peter could not figure it out, but John was beginning to.

> So the other disciple who had come first to the tomb entered then also, and he *saw* and believed. For as yet they did not understand the Scripture, that He must rise again from the dead. So the disciples went away again to their own homes. (vv. 8–10, emphasis added)

This time the word *saw, eiden* in Greek,[10] means "to perceive," "to realize."[11] In other words, it all fell into place, it clicked. John stood next to Peter gazing at that odd sight, and the light came on. "Peter, Peter, He's been raised from the dead! He's alive!" John may not have understood Jesus' Resurrection as foretold by Scripture (v. 9), but what he saw, he believed.

7. Blum, "John," in *The Bible Knowledge Commentary*, p. 342.

8. Merrill C. Tenney, *The Reality of the Resurrection* (New York, N.Y.: Harper and Row, Publishers, 1963), pp. 118–19.

9. Merrill C. Tenney, *John: The Gospel of Belief* (1976; reprint, Grand Rapids, Mich.: William B. Eerdmans Publishing Co., 1989), p. 281.

10. Blum, "John," in *The Bible Knowledge Commentary*, p. 342.

11. Kittel and Friedrich, eds., *Theological Dictionary of the New Testament*, p. 710.

Living Insights

Frank Morison was a well-educated British lawyer, his thinking shaped by the German critics, Oxford professor Matthew Arnold, and biologist Dr. Thomas Huxley—all of whom openly denied even the possibility of miracles.

Morison, in an effort to disprove the Christian belief that Jesus was miraculously raised from the dead, set out to write a book. Little did he suspect that the book he ended up writing would be so radically different from the book he had planned. *Who Moved the Stone?* turned out to be a defense of the bodily resurrection of Christ. In his own words, he "discovered one day that not only could he no longer write the book as he had once conceived it, but that he would not if he could."[12] And this change of heart happened, "not suddenly, as in a flash of insight or inspiration, but slowly, almost imperceptibly, by the very stubbornness of the facts themselves."[13]

Not all of us have been hard-core skeptics like Morison, but some of us have needed to be convinced by hard, cold evidence. We must not stop there, though. Christ's Resurrection is spiritual truth, not impersonal data to be analyzed, filed away, and kept at a distance. It's living truth—a turning point in history that reverberates through each and every age and through each and every believer. It is meant to travel through our heads, to our hearts, and out into our lives.

Let's begin, then, as Morison did, thinking through Jesus' Resurrection. We'll then move this spiritual truth to our hearts and out into our lives in the Living Insights in the next chapter. Take some time to examine what the Holy Spirit revealed to the other writers of Scripture about what that empty tomb of our living Lord has accomplished and is accomplishing in our lives.

Acts 13:30–39 _____

_____

_____

_____

Romans 1:1–4 _____

_____

---

12. Frank Morison, *Who Moved the Stone?* (Downers Grove, Ill.: InterVarsity Press, 1971), preface.
13. Morison, *Who Moved the Stone?*, preface.

Romans 6:1–14 _____

1 Corinthians 15:12–23, 42–49 _____

1 Corinthians 15:50–58 _____

2 Corinthians 4:14 _____

Ephesians 1:18–23; 2:6 _____

Colossians 2:9–12 _____

Colossians 3:1–4 _____

1 Peter 1:3–5 _____

1 Peter 1:18–21 _____

Because of Jesus' Resurrection, we can rejoice with Paul: "Death is swallowed up in victory. O death, where is your victory? O death, where is your sting?" (1 Cor. 15:54b–55)! This triumph over death is not just a future hope for us, but as we shall see, it is our hope each and every day.

Chapter 13

Reactions to the Resurrected Lord

John 20:11–31

An empty tomb.

This is all Mary Magdalene saw. This is all she understood.

Her Lord, who had freed her from the living death of having seven demons (see Luke 8:2), had been betrayed and brutalized, murdered and entombed. And now He couldn't even rest in peace—His body was missing! Some mysterious "they" had taken Him out of the tomb, and she didn't know where He was (John 20:2).

Now she couldn't have the comfort of tenderly anointing His body. Now she couldn't say her final good-bye. He was gone, desecrated, nowhere to be found.

Jesus, though, was nearer than she knew. And soon she would have greater comfort than she could ever imagine, and there would be no more good-byes . . . forever.

I. Observations about the Passage

When Jesus' tomb was found empty, the first fear, voiced by Mary, was that He'd been kidnapped (John 20:2). But after Peter and John investigated the scene, they came to a different conclusion (vv. 8–10). While all the pieces of this puzzling event hadn't fallen into place yet, these two disciples saw enough to get a clear picture: the missing piece was the resurrected Christ. The first sighting of Him occurred early Sunday morning (vv. 11–17); the second, that evening (vv. 19–23); the third, eight days later (vv. 26–29). The people who saw Him were Mary Magdalene, the disciples, and Thomas. Another observation of the passage is that the literary structure of each sighting is similar. There is an appearance of the risen Christ, a reaction to that appearance, and a statement made by Christ.

II. Encounters with the Risen Christ

The first person Jesus sought to appear to was the grieving Mary Magdalene, and we can imagine the delight He took in turning her sorrow to joy.

Parts of this chapter have been adapted from the study guide *The Majesty of God's Son,* from the Bible-teaching ministry of Charles R. Swindoll (Anaheim, Calif.: Insight for Living, 1999), pp. 133, 134.

A. Mary Magdalene. Troubled and confused, Mary stands at the mouth of the empty tomb, weeping so much that she doesn't see the miracle in front of her, doesn't seem to realize that she's talking with angels.

> But Mary was standing outside the tomb weeping; and so, as she wept, she stooped and looked into the tomb; and she beheld two angels in white sitting, one at the head, and one at the feet, where the body of Jesus had been lying. And they said to her, "Woman, why are you weeping?" She said to them, "Because they have taken away my Lord, and I do not know where they have laid Him." (vv. 11–13)

Maybe it is hazy or foggy on this morning . . . maybe tears blur her eyes . . . maybe Jesus is the last person she expects to see. But when she turns around, she doesn't recognize the One for whom her heart is aching.

> When she had said this, she turned around, and beheld Jesus standing there, and did not know that it was Jesus. Jesus said to her, "Woman, why are you weeping? Whom are you seeking?" Supposing Him to be the gardener, she said to Him, "Sir, if you have carried Him away, tell me where you have laid Him, and I will take Him away." (vv. 14–15)

Jesus first kindly addresses Mary as "woman." She still doesn't recognize His voice, though. But when He calls her by name, He immediately comes into focus.

> Jesus said to her, "Mary!" She turned and said to Him in Hebrew, "Rabboni!" (which means, Teacher). (v. 16)

Although not explicitly stated, the next verse implies that Mary, overcome with joy, falls at Jesus' feet and clings to Him for all she's worth. Gently but firmly, Jesus urges her to let go—this won't be the only time she sees Him, and besides, there are others who are still mourning and need to hear the good news. So Jesus bestows on Mary the privilege of telling the disciples that He is alive!

> Jesus said to her, "Stop clinging to Me, for I have not yet ascended to the Father; but go to My brethren, and say to them, 'I ascend to My Father and your Father, and My God and your God.'" (v. 17)

Do you notice the subtle shift in Jesus' choice of words? In the Upper Room, He had called His disciples His friends (15:15). Now they are His brothers, sharing the same Father, "become children of God" (1:12). And this new relationship, made possible by Jesus' Resurrection, is available to all who believe in Him. Her heart overflowing with joy, Mary runs to do as her Lord has asked.

Mary Magdalene came, announcing to the disciples, "I have seen the Lord," and that He had said these things to her. (20:18)

B. The disciples. Abruptly, John cuts to another scene. The room is dark, with only a flickering oil lamp dancing shadows upon the walls. With windows shuttered and door barred, the disciples huddle together, afraid of what the Jewish officials might do to them after seeing what they did to Jesus. But Jesus Himself pierces their gloom.

When therefore it was evening, on that day, the first day of the week, and when the doors were shut where the disciples were, for fear of the Jews, Jesus came and stood in their midst, and said to them, "Peace be with you." (v. 19)

When they first see Jesus, these fearful disciples turn pale as ghosts (compare Luke 24:37). Did they not believe Mary? Apparently not, according to Mark (Mark 16:11). Not even Peter and John's inspection of the empty tomb and grave clothes prepared them for seeing Jesus alive. But with Jesus' words "Peace be with you," a calm settles over their hearts. And they gather the courage to come near their Lord.

And when He had said this, He showed them both His hands and His side. The disciples therefore rejoiced when they saw the Lord. Jesus therefore said to them again, "Peace be with you; as the Father has sent Me, I also send you." And when He had said this, He breathed on them, and said to them, "Receive the Holy Spirit. If you forgive the sins of any, their sins have been forgiven them; if you retain the sins of any, they have been retained." (John 20:20–23)

"Peace be with you . . . Peace be with you," Jesus tells His fearful disciples not once, but twice (vv. 19, 21). Bruce Milne tells us,

Shalom basically means "well-being" in its fullest sense. It gathers up all the blessings of the kingdom of God; shalom is life at its best under the gracious hand of God. Jesus' use of it on that Easter evening therefore represented the first truly authentic bestowal of shalom in the history of the world! . . . For the peace of reconciliation and life from God is now imparted.[1]

1. Bruce Milne, *The Message of John: Here Is Your King!*, The Bible Speaks Today Series (Downers Grove, Ill.: InterVarsity Press, 1993), p. 297.

As the Father sent Jesus to show and tell the world of God's redeeming love, so now Jesus also commissions His disciples to go and do the same. He breathes on them the Spirit, until the Spirit will fully indwell them at Pentecost (see Acts 2). And He gives them their message: Jesus has provided for the forgiveness of sins for all who believe in Him, but those who do not will remain in their sins. The apostle Paul later summed up their assignment:

> God . . . reconciled us to Himself through Christ, and gave us the ministry of reconciliation. . . . We are ambassadors for Christ. (2 Cor. 5:18b, 20a)

C. Thomas. One disciple, however, wasn't present for this radiant, empowering encounter with the risen Lord: Thomas.

> But Thomas, one of the twelve, called Didymus, was not with them when Jesus came. The other disciples therefore were saying to him, "We have seen the Lord!" But he said to them, "Unless I shall see in His hands the imprint of the nails, and put my finger into the place of the nails, and put my hand into His side, I will not believe." (20:24–25)

For eight days after this event (see v. 26), the other disciples were joyously linked in the experience they had shared. Thomas must have felt like such an outsider. He wanted to believe, but he hadn't been there. Where he *had* been was on the hill that Friday. What he *had* seen was the body, hanging limp on the cross. The skepticism and logic that may have been his natural approach to life kept him shaking his head: "Wishful thinking. It's what we'd all like to be true." Graciously, Jesus gives Thomas the proof he needs. And notice, His words are gentle, direct, and, above all, convincing.

> And after eight days again His disciples were inside, but Thomas with them. Jesus came, the doors having been shut, and stood in their midst and said, "Peace be with you." Then He said to Thomas, "Reach here your finger, and see My hands; and reach here your hand and put it into my side; and be not unbelieving, but believing. Thomas answered and said to Him, "My Lord and my God!" (vv. 26–28)

With these words, Thomas uttered the climactic words of John's Gospel. For John's purpose in writing his Gospel was

> so that you may believe that Jesus is the Christ, the Son of God; and that believing you may have life in His name. (v. 31)

III. Practical Application

Jesus did make one other important comment to Thomas: "Because you have seen Me, have you believed? Blessed are they who did not see, and yet believed." (v. 29) Only a select few saw Jesus in His risen state before He ascended to heaven. And those few who saw and believed, including Thomas, have spread the Good News "to the remotest part of the earth" and to all generations throughout time (Acts 1:8). They have given us their eyewitness testimony—this is what John's Gospel is. We depend on those to whom Jesus physically revealed Himself—we take by faith that their testimony is true. And through the aid of the Spirit, we believe and receive eternal life. So trust is our way of life, and our trust is what Jesus Himself blessed. Trust is not easy, though, and some, like Thomas, will struggle with doubt. If this describes you, don't be discouraged. Instead, take your doubts to Jesus, just as Thomas did.

Some people need to doubt before they believe. If doubt leads to questions, questions lead to answers, and the answers are accepted, then doubt has done good work. It is when doubt becomes stubbornness and stubbornness becomes a life-style that doubt harms faith. When you doubt, don't stop there. Let your doubt deepen your faith as you continue to search for the answer.[2]

Holding onto Faith

In C. S. Lewis' classic *The Screwtape Letters,* Uncle Screwtape, a seasoned devil, corresponds with his nephew Wormwood, a fledgling young devil on his first assignment to earth. In his advice, Screwtape refers to God as the "Enemy" and offers some keen insight into the subject of God's children living by faith.

He wants them to learn to walk and must therefore take away His hand; and if only the will to walk is really there He is pleased even with their stumbles. Do not be deceived, Wormwood. Our cause is never more in danger than when a human, no longer desiring, but still intending, to do our Enemy's will, looks round upon a universe from which every trace of Him seems to have vanished, and asks why he has been forsaken, and still obeys.[3]

---

2. Bruce B. Barton, Philip W. Comfort, David R. Veerman, and Neil Wilson, *John,* Life Application Bible Commentary Series (Wheaton, Ill.: Tyndale House Publishers, 1993), p. 399.

3. C. S. Lewis, *The Screwtape Letters* (New York, N.Y.: The Macmillan Co., 1959), p. 47.

Living Insights

In our last chapter's Living Insights, we examined and thought through the reality and spiritual privileges that Jesus' Resurrection secures for us. Now let's bring those thoughts into our hearts and learn how His rising works itself out in our lives.

First, consider what life would be like if Jesus had not risen. If He had simply died, we probably never would have heard of Him. He would have been just another martyr, just another victim of injustice, just another lost cause in the world's parade of martyrs, victims, and lost causes.

But He did rise—death is not the end of His story! Because He rose,

> Good overcame evil!
> Light overtook darkness!
> Love overthrew hate!
> Life overwhelmed death!

The Resurrection did not, however, nullify, undo, or in any way wipe out the Crucifixion. On the contrary, Jesus' rising affirmed and confirmed not only what was accomplished on the Cross but the very way of the Cross. Because Jesus is now the ever-living One, we know that everything He said is the truth and that the life He showed us is the true way. He *did* come from God, He *is* the Lord of heaven and earth, and Love *will* have the final say. This is the solid hope we need to take into our hearts! This is the dependable direction that can lead our lives!

Author N. T. Wright reflects on the risen and reigning Jesus, whom John more fully reveals in his last book, Revelation:

> Revelation begins with a vision of the risen Jesus (1.12–16). Snow-white hair, eyes of fire, feet of polished bronze, voice like a waterfall, and his face like the sun itself —no wonder John fell at his feet as though he was dead. This is where terror and joy meet: this is the Easter Jesus. "Don't be afraid," he says; *"I am the first and the last, and the living one. I died, and look, I am alive for evermore."* "And"—and this sounds almost conspiratorial—*"I've got the keys—the keys of Death and Hades"* (1.17–18). What-ever you've lost; whoever you've lost; whatever bits of your life are locked away for sorrow or shame, I've got the keys.[4]

---

4. N. T. Wright, *Following Jesus: Biblical Reflections on Discipleship* (Grand Rapids, Mich.: William B. Eerdmans Publishing Co., 1994), p. 55.

Let's pause here to make this personal. Are there sins, or past shames, that have locked away parts of your life? You don't have to write them down if you would rather not. They may be for Jesus' eyes only, and that's OK. But if you would like to, we've provided you the space to do that.

_____

_____

_____

_____

_____

_____

_____

If they're still haunting you, keeping you trapped, stop right now and pray. Bring them to the risen Christ. Jesus is not the one who accuses—that's Satan ("accuser" is the root meaning of his name). Jesus is the One who wants your freedom and salvation so badly that He gave His own life for you. He has condemned your accuser and set you in His grace (see Rev. 12:10–11a). His love and His power to forgive are greater than any sin, accusation, or condemnation. Remember, He did not come to call the righteous, but sinners, that He might save them (see Matt. 9:13; 1 Tim. 1:15).

Ask Him to help you let go of what entraps you through guilt. Ask Him to make His forgiveness real to you. Take your time.

Wright also tells us that "Easter is all about the wiping away of tears.

> . . . In this new-heaven-and-new-earth there are several things that will have no more place. . . . There will be no sin, nothing that corrupts and defaces the human reflection of the living God. There will be no death; no mourning; no pain. The tyrant's weapons will all have gone. *And so God will wipe away all tears from all eyes.* Yes, Mary; your tears will be dried. Yes, Peter, yours will be wiped away. . . . The tears of the Belfast widow will be wiped away. The tears of the Rwandan orphan will be dried. The weeping of the abandoned lover, the bitter tears of the man who's lost his job, the tears of the black

child snubbed in the white school, the tears we cry in secret and the tears we cry in our hearts, all will be wiped away.

And it is all because of the Lamb . . . who by his blood defeated evil, and rescued human beings and the world from its tyranny. . . . The wrath of the Lamb, of which Revelation speaks from time to time, is the anger of love against all that hurts and damages the beloved. The *love* of the Lamb is the great reality that undergirds the entire vision.

And it is that love which is revealed at Easter.[5]

Do you have tears you need the risen Lamb to wipe away? He is no tyrant, who inflicts pain for the pleasure of it. He is a gentle and humble and righteous ruler, a King who washes His servants' feet. Take some time now to pour out your heart to Him, in writing or in private prayer, and let Him wipe away your tears. Trust Him, wait on Him, to turn your sorrow to joy.

_____

_____

_____

_____

_____

_____

_____

As a believer in the risen Lamb, do you know what you are now? You are part of the community of "Sunday people called to live in a world of Fridays . . . Easter people, called to minister to a world full of Calvarys."[6] You are an Easter person! So where Christ has wiped away your tears, you are to wipe away others' tears. You are called to comfort others as God has comforted you (see 2 Cor. 1:3–5). You are called to help reconcile people to God and live in His peace (5:18–19). You are called to overcome evil with good (Rom. 12:21). And you are called to supersede fear with faith.

5. Wright, *Following Jesus,* pp. 58, 60–61.
6. Wright, *Following Jesus,* p. 61.

The resurrection of Jesus issues the surprising command: don't be afraid; because the God who made the world is the God who raised Jesus from the dead, and calls you now to follow him. Believing in the resurrection of Jesus isn't just a matter of believing that certain things are true about the physical body of Jesus that had been crucified. These truths are vital and nonnegotiable, but they point beyond themselves, to the God who was responsible for them. Believing in this God means believing that it is going to be all right; and this belief, is, ultimately, incompatible with fear. As John says in his letter, perfect love casts out fear (1 John 4.18). And the resurrection is the revelation of perfect love, God's perfect love for us, his human creatures.[7]

So, what does Jesus' Resurrection mean for us in our daily life? That our shame, sorrow, and fear are conquered *now*—although God knows it will take us the rest of our lives to grow into realizing this truth. Nevertheless, because of Easter, the hope of heaven is ours—and the life of heaven doesn't have to wait for a future glorious day. It's ours to begin living now!

7. Wright, *Following Jesus*, p. 68.

Chapter 14

Coming to Terms with Your Calling

John 21:1–17

Gone Fishing.

How many times have you wanted to hang that sign on your door? Maybe when there's a lull in business. Maybe when job pressures hem you in and you feel trapped. Or maybe when a wave of nostalgia washes over you one warm summer day and you yearn to go barefoot at the old fishing hole where so many fond memories are pooled.

Maybe those were some of the disciples' thoughts after Jesus died. Perhaps that's why they took the day off and went fishing. The ministry, for all practical purposes, had shut down. Sure, the Resurrection brought a flurry of renewed optimism, but it also raised a number of questions they had no answers for—like, "Now what?"

Perhaps the disciples felt hemmed in by the impending threat of the Roman government. After all, Jesus had warned them that if the world persecuted Him, it would certainly persecute them too.

Perhaps, as they sat by the Sea of Galilee and listened to the rhythm of the waves, they felt their spirits ebbing nostalgically back to the past. When Peter said "I'm going fishing," thoughts of his past came back to him—thoughts of when Jesus first recruited him.

> And as He was going along by the Sea of Galilee, He saw Simon and Andrew, the brother of Simon, casting a net in the sea; for they were fishermen. And Jesus said to them, "Follow Me, and I will make you become fishers of men." And they immediately left the nets and followed Him. And going on a little farther, He saw James the son of Zebedee, and John his brother, who were also in the boat mending the nets. And immediately He called them; and they left their father Zebedee in the boat with the hired servants, and went away to follow Him. (Mark 1:16–20)

For the next three years these fishermen learned from Jesus, watching Him calm storms, walk on water, cast His saving net into humanity's sea. But now, in the wake of His death and in the anticipation of His return to the Father, all was calm, and the disciples returned to their old vocation—back to Galilee and their nets. It is there we find them in John 21.

I. The Disciples Alone

The scene opens on the shores of Galilee's sea, also known as the Sea of Tiberias.

> After these things Jesus manifested Himself again to the disciples at the Sea of Tiberias, and He manifested Himself in this way. There were together Simon Peter, and Thomas called Didymus, and Nathanael of Cana in Galilee, and the sons of Zebedee, and two others of His disciples. (John 21:1–2)

The disciples find themselves quietly enveloped in melancholy darkness. Few words are spoken. No one knows what to say. One of them skips a rock. Another mindlessly picks up a handful of sand and sifts it through his fingers. Finally, Peter breaks the silence.

> Simon Peter said to them, "I am going fishing." They said to him, "We will also come with you." They went out, and got into the boat; and that night they caught nothing. (v. 3)

There was nothing sinful in what the disciples did. They were probably confused, without clear direction. Ever been there yourself? Are you standing on a similar shore right now, casting nets in some quiet cove, away from the mainstream God has called you to? If so, you may need a visit from Jesus, like the one in the following verses.

II. Jesus and the Disciples

How frustrated the disciples must have felt when time after time their nets came up empty.

A. The manifestation. At the height of their frustration and exhaustion, Jesus quietly appears to them.

> But when the day was now breaking, Jesus stood on the beach; yet the disciples did not know that it was Jesus. Jesus therefore said to them, "Children, you do not have any fish, do you?" They answered Him, "No." And He said to them, "Cast the net on the right-hand side of the boat, and you will find a catch." They cast therefore, and then they were not able to haul it in because of the great number of fish. (vv. 4–6)

Barren . . . or Bearing Fruit?

Earlier in the Gospel, Jesus had told the disciples: "I am the vine, you are the branches; he who abides in Me, and I in him, he bears much fruit; for apart from Me you can do nothing" (15:5).

113

> Did these words echo in the disciples' minds each time they brought up an empty net? How empty, how futile our lives can be when Christ is left out. When our calling is ignored, we can't sell, we can't teach, we can't counsel, we can't clean house, we can't function fruitfully—period—even in our vocation. The disciples were fishermen by trade, and they couldn't even catch a minnow. Are your nets coming up empty?
>
> Are you burning the midnight oil and getting nothing but burned out? Maybe the Lord is calling to you from the shore. If so, take a minute to listen. He might lead you to the catch of a lifetime!

Imagine the disciples' surprise when they pull up the net brimming with fish, each one a keeper (21:11). The exuberance of the catch causes Peter to pause and remember another time when they were surprised by an incredible catch of fish . . . when Peter first realized who Jesus really was. As he stands there in that little fishing boat, the memory begins to vividly come back to him.

> Now it came about that while the multitude were pressing around [Jesus] and listening to the word of God, He was standing by the lake of Gennesaret; and He saw two boats lying at the edge of the lake; but the fishermen had gotten out of them, and were washing their nets. And He got into one of the boats, which was Simon's, and asked him to put out a little way from the land. And He sat down and began teaching the multitudes from the boat. And when He had finished speaking, He said to Simon, "Put out into the deep water and let down your nets for a catch." And Simon answered and said, "Master, we worked hard all night and caught nothing, but at Your bidding I will let down the nets." And when they had done this, they enclosed a great quantity of fish; and their nets began to break; and they signaled to their partners in the other boat, for them to come and help them. And they came, and filled both of the boats, so that they began to sink. But when Simon Peter saw that, he fell down at Jesus' feet, saying, "Depart from me, for I am a sinful man, O Lord!" (Luke 5:1–8)

Suddenly Peter's memory is brought into sharper relief by John.

> That disciple therefore whom Jesus loved said to

Peter, "It is the Lord." And so when Simon Peter heard that it was the Lord, he put his outer garment on (for he was stripped for work), and threw himself into the sea. (John 21:7)

Rather than wanting the Lord to depart from him, Peter swims the fastest one-hundred-yard freestyle ever seen in order to reach the Savior. Straining at the oars and the net, the others follow Peter.

But the other disciples came in the little boat, for they were not far from the land, but about one hundred yards away, dragging the net full of fish. (v. 8)

B. The invitation. As Peter and the other disciples reach the shore, they find the meal prepared and the table set. This was no chance meeting but one carefully planned by the Lord.

And so when they got out upon the land, they saw a charcoal fire already laid, and fish placed on it, and bread. Jesus said to them, "Bring some of the fish which you have now caught." Simon Peter went up, and drew the net to land, full of large fish, a hundred and fifty-three; and although there were so many, the net was not torn. Jesus said to them, "Come and have breakfast." None of the disciples ventured to question Him, "Who are You?" knowing that it was the Lord. (vv. 9–12)

C. The conversation. As in days past, the disciples sit with Jesus, eating and talking together. Their voices murmur across the stretch of deserted beach. Smoke curls above the fire. The heat of the glowing coals begins to chase away the morning chill. It's an intimate moment. Every word that falls from Jesus' lips feeds their hungry hearts. His presence reminds them of that which they had momentarily been stalled in—their calling. How gracious of the Lord to step into our own sphere of influence—our jobs—and remind us that He still wants us to carry out our calling. To be involved in a vocation without a calling is to settle for a life of empty nets.[1]

III. Jesus and Simon Peter

As the sun dawns on that placid sea and the disciples warm themselves by the fire, Jesus opens a recent wound in Peter's life.

So when they had finished breakfast, Jesus said to Simon Peter, "Simon, son of John, do you love Me more than these?" He said to Him, "Yes, Lord; You know that I

---

1. Daniel's life perfectly illustrates a blending of the two—faithfulness in work (Dan. 6:1–2) and consistency in calling (vv. 3–4).

love You." He said to him, "Tend My lambs." He said to him again a second time, "Simon, son of John, do you love Me?" He said to Him, "Yes, Lord; You know that I love You." He said to him, "Shepherd My sheep." He said to him the third time, "Simon, son of John, do you love Me?" Peter was grieved because He said to him the third time, "Do you love Me?" And he said to Him, "Lord, You know all things; You know that I love You." Jesus said to him, "Tend My sheep." (vv. 15–17)

Three times Jesus asks the same question—one question for each time Peter denied Him. Notice that Jesus doesn't call him Peter, the rock, but Simon. With the name Simon, Jesus takes Peter back to the start of their relationship and begins to rebuild the foundation. The first question Jesus asks is, "Do you love Me more than these?" The word *these* isn't identified; it could mean "these men," referring to the disciples, or it could mean "these fish," referring to his vocation. Possibly it refers to both. The Greek word for "love" here is *agapaō*, the highest form of love. Peter's reaction, however, does not include the word *agapaō*, but *phileō*, the word for friendship: "You know I'm fond of You; we're friends." The commission of Christ is clear: "Tend My lambs." In repeating the question, Jesus sensitively drops the phrase "more than these." This takes the pressure off and allows Peter to search his heart to see where the Lord really fits in his life. Again the commission, "Shepherd My sheep." In the final question, Jesus uses the same term for love that Peter has used—*phileō*; "Simon, are you fond of Me?" Peter is grieved; yet he is honest about where the relationship is: "You know that I am fond of You . . . You know that I have a flawed love." The remarkable thing is that Christ's commission remains consistent: "In spite of that, I *still* want you to tend My sheep. I haven't given up on you. I haven't put you on the shelf."

Coming to Terms with Your Calling

Whether you preach from the pulpit on Sunday morning or pump gas on the corner Monday, God wants to blend your vocation with your calling. Your vocation is special, and your calling is sacred, regardless of whether you wear a clerical collar or a blue collar. No matter what job pays the bills, God wants you to come to terms with your calling and use your job to further His kingdom.

Take a minute to evaluate your priorities: Exactly where does Jesus Christ fit in your Monday-through-Saturday lifestyle? He is asking you today the same question He asked Peter: "Do you love Me more than these?" Do you? If so, you'll find a way to tend His sheep, even while you work.

 Living Insights

Did you ever wonder why Jesus still had the scars in His hands, feet, and sides after the Resurrection? Why weren't these wounds made like new, erased?

Maybe it's because they are the marks of His love. They are the scars of our salvation. They are the wounds of our healing, as Isaiah foretold and Peter himself echoed:

> By his wounds we are healed. (Isa. 53:5 NIV)

> He Himself bore our sins in His body on the cross, that we might die to sin and live to righteousness; for by His wounds you were healed. (1 Pet. 2:24)

And maybe, as Jesus' restoration of Peter suggests, through our wounds He can heal others (compare 2 Cor. 1:3–4).

Our failures and our hurts don't disqualify us from serving Jesus. They don't put us on the sidelines of the work of His kingdom. Jesus isn't our accuser, remember, but our restorer, forgiver, healer, and Savior. He is the One who makes all things new (2 Cor. 5:17). Lesslie Newbigin makes these observations from Jesus' dialogue with Peter:

> The threefold denial is wiped out and forgiven in the threefold commissioning. Yet the record is one more reminder that the flock which belongs to Jesus consists not of the righteous but of sinners called to repentance. If Peter has a primacy among the apostles, it is because he has primacy as a forgiven sinner. "You are Peter" is said to the one to whom in the next breath Jesus will say, "Get behind me, Satan" (Matt. 16:18, 23). It is to the fisherman overwhelmed by the realization of his sinfulness that Jesus says, "Do not be afraid; henceforth you will be catching men" (Luke 5:8–10). It is to the disciple who will fall away that Jesus says, "When you have turned again, strengthen your brethren" (Luke 22:31f).[2]

---

2. Lesslie Newbigin, *The Light Has Come: An Exposition of the Fourth Gospel* (Grand Rapids, Mich.: William B. Eerdmans Publishing Co., 1982), p. 279.

Are there any failures, mistakes, sins, or wounds in your life that you feel disqualify you from Christ's calling to be a witness of His Good News? What have you done about them? What impact are they having on your life?

_____

_____

_____

_____

Have you repented of them? Have you brought your imperfect self to Christ and told Him that you love Him and want Him to use you in any way He can? Or is something stopping you from doing that? What would that be? Take that to Him now, won't you, and let Him help you leave it behind.

_____

_____

_____

_____

In Christ's restoring hands, how do you think He can use your wounds to heal others? What good can He bring out of your woundedness? Consider, for example, qualities such as compassion, humility, courage, sympathy, wisdom, sensitivity, patience, a softer heart. What has He done and what do you see Him doing with hurts that may have scarred you?

_____

_____

_____

_____

None of us is perfect, but all of us can be forgiven and consecrated for Jesus' use. In our own strength, parts of our lives look very much like broken shards of glass, cracked by life and our own poor choices. But in His hands, we're more like pieces of stained glass, our broken lives melded together with other broken people, to become a window of God's love through which His radiant light can shine in unspeakable beauty.

Chapter 15

" . . . And What about This Man?"

John 21:17–23

Did you ever play "Follow the Leader" when you were a kid? One child would get to be the leader, and everyone else would have to do exactly as the leader did, following single file. You might wind up having to climb a fence, swing on a tree, or hop on one foot all the way up the block. And do you remember what would happen if somebody took their eyes off the leader? It would throw everyone else off, and you'd usually end up bumping into each other and toppling like a stack of dominoes!

Well, Jesus hasn't called us to be human dominoes, tripping up ourselves and others when we take our eyes off of Him. Bumbling Keystone Kristians we are not! But diligent disciples we are. In these last few verses of John's Gospel, that's Jesus message to Peter and to us. As Peter takes his eyes off Jesus and cranes his neck to see about John, Jesus snaps him to attention with an urgent, "Follow Me!"

I. Eavesdropping on Jesus and Peter

John 21 forms an epilogue to the Gospel. And like any well-written ending, it is saturated with meaning. From verses 17–23, we'll wring as much as we possibly can. In each section—loving and serving (v. 17), living and dying (vv. 18–19a), lingering and following (vv. 19b–23)—Jesus teaches Peter a significant lesson the disciple has not learned before.

A. Loving and serving.
From our last study we learned that Jesus singled Peter out and asked him three searching questions, each focusing on Peter's love for Him. You can almost feel the pain from Jesus' poignant words: "Do you love Me?" In Peter's mind, he was a failure . . . a loser . . . a washout. As he sat on the shore listening to Jesus, Peter felt as insignificant as a piece of driftwood about to be fed to the campfire. But when he realized he was not going to be used for kindling but for building Christ's church, he learned a valuable lesson: *Past failures can be forgiven in love.*

The People God Uses

Have you ever stopped to think about the people God uses to accomplish His purposes? The heavy hitters, right? Noah . . . Abraham . . . Moses . . . David . . .

119

Elijah . . . Jonah . . . Peter. Yet all of them failed; and some, tragically.

When we fail, Satan is quick to run us into the ground and trample any remaining vestige of self-worth. He'll have us call ourselves every name in the book: fool, idiot, loser, failure.

But love "does not take into account a wrong suffered" (1 Cor. 13:5b). Jesus doesn't sit in heaven sharpening His red pencil to jot down every time we fall on our face. Peter himself tells us, years later, that "love covers a multitude of sins" (1 Pet. 4:8). And where did he learn that lesson? Right on that beach where Jesus picked him up and dusted him off.

You've been there too, haven't you? You've failed Him. You've fallen flat on your face. When you're down there with sand in your eyes and mouth, remember: Satan is the one who's going to kick you while you're down. Jesus will be there reaching out His hand to pick you up.

B. Living and dying. Still speaking to Peter, Jesus informs him of a contrast that would occur in his life.

> "Truly, truly, I say to you, when you were younger, you used to gird yourself, and walk wherever you wished; but when you grow old, you will stretch out your hands, and someone else will gird you, and bring you where you do not wish to go." Now this He said, signifying by what kind of death he would glorify God. (John 21:18–19a)

The picture Jesus paints in the first part of verse 18 is that of a self-assured youth, strong-willed, capable, determined, and independent. But in the latter part of that verse, the picture changes radically. The strong self-will has been replaced by submission, a readiness to follow the Savior anywhere, even to death. In the third volume of Eusebius' *Ecclesiastical History,* the first-century historian notes that Peter was martyred around A.D. 61. First, he saw his wife crucified before his very eyes, and then, with a willing heart, he submitted himself to the cross. But feeling unworthy to die in the same manner as his Lord, he asked that he be crucified upside down instead. What a lesson Peter was to learn as he stood on that shore: *Present lifestyle is no guarantee of the same future.*

C. Lingering and following. Peter is learning some timely lessons. But perhaps Jesus is saving the best one for last, in John 21:19–23.

> Now this He said, signifying by what kind of death he would glorify God. And when He had spoken this, He said to him, "Follow Me!" Peter, turning around, saw the disciple whom Jesus loved following them; the one who also had leaned back on His breast at the supper, and said, "Lord, who is the one who betrays You?" Peter therefore seeing him said to Jesus, "Lord, and what about this man?" (vv. 19–21)

Jesus and Peter are starting to walk away from the group huddled around the campfire that morning. Looking over his shoulder, Peter sees John walking behind them. So typical of human nature, Peter's mental wheels begin to churn on the grist of a thought: "And what about John?" Like a charcoaled ember inflamed by a fanning breeze, an old weakness of Peter's suddenly flares up. Habitually trying to manage things, Peter sticks his nose into somebody else's business. In doing so, he tries to compare his future to John's. Jesus' response is a terse "mind your own business."

> Jesus said to him, "If I want him to remain until I come, what is that to you? You follow Me!" (v. 22)

The lesson comes through loud and clear: *Personal obedience is an individual matter.*

Comparing Brings Confusion

When Jesus asks Peter, "What is that to you?" (v. 22), He is trying to teach the disciple a valuable lesson: God doesn't deal with us on a comparative basis but on an individual one. He redeems us individually. He rebukes us individually. He rewards us individually.

"Follow Me!" That's the challenge put to Peter. Not to follow John or the rest of the disciples or the majority, but "Me!"

And if you try to follow Jesus while looking over your shoulder to see what direction other Christians are going, sooner or later you're going to stub your toe or stray into a tree.

No, you can only *follow* Him if your eyes are fixed on Him—Him and only Him.

II. Summarizing the Applications

Peter learned three lessons on that early-morning Galilee beach. With regard to the past, he learned not to quit. With regard to the future, he learned not to predict. And regarding the present, he learned not to compare. One final thing: verse 23 states that there later arose some confusion about Christ's words to Peter.

> This saying therefore went out among the brethren that that disciple would not die; yet Jesus did not say to him that he would not die, but only, "If I want him to remain until I come, what is that to you?"

Apparently this conversation got garbled in first-century gossip. People evidently thought that John would not die before Christ returned! This leads us to a concluding application: *People often misunderstand God's message.* When that happens, as it inevitably will, don't be concerned. Some things are just between you and God, and some people will never fully understand what He has revealed only to you in the quietness of your heart.

Living Insights

"Don't worry about John, Peter," Jesus told His ever-so-human disciple, "You look at Me!" Can you identify with Peter? Who of us can't! Take a moment to examine this area of your life in the light of Jesus' words.

Do you sometimes find yourself spending more time investigating what God is doing in someone else's life than giving attention to what He has called you to do? Does your curiosity ever get out of hand? What happens? What does God need to do to get your eyes back on Him?

_____

_____

_____

_____

_____

_____

The apostle Paul has a name for this activity. He also has some instructions for dealing with it. Look up 2 Thessalonians 3:11b–13, and tailor his advice to your situation.

_____

_____

_____

_____

_____

Quite often, our curiosity about God's will in another person's life can degenerate into comparison. Comparing can cause us to feel like we don't measure up, and then we don't value the gifts and unique purpose God has given us. Or we can feel proud, thinking we're hot stuff and everyone else is cold leftovers. Comparing can turn into competing, and this comes at the expense of compassion.

Is there someone, or perhaps a particular group of people, you find that you compare yourself with? What effect does this have on you—do you devalue yourself or devalue others? Or does it just make you unsure of what Christ has called you to do?

_____

_____

_____

_____

_____

_____

_____

Paul again has some counsel for us in Romans 12:3–8; 1 Corinthians 12:14–26; and Galatians 6:4. Prayerfully think through these passages, and summarize Paul's advice to you.

_____

_____

_____

_____

_____

_____

The worst thing about nosiness and comparison is that they take our eyes off Christ. We get so busy looking at everybody else that we can begin to follow the crowd instead of Christ. And then we let slip from our hands the unique job He has called us to do. As you take into your life Jesus' lesson for Peter, let Bruce Milne's wise words help shape your thoughts.

The personal relationship between the Lord and individual Christians, including issues like the future form and sphere of their service, the degree of their obedience, or the quality of their contribution, is "holy ground," sacred to the individuals concerned. We may not walk there unless with express invitation or clear obligation, and even then only with the greatest sensitivity and reserve. The ministries of Peter and John would be different. Peter would be the shepherd, John the seer; Peter the preacher, John the penman; Peter the foundational witness, John the faithful writer; Peter would die in the agony and passion of martyrdom, John would live on to great age and pass away in quiet serenity.

Peter is faced here, as we all are, with the fact of partnership in following Jesus. There are many others on the road with us, as truly Christ's, as surely commissioned, as deeply loved, as greatly valued. Their calling and gifts may be different; their instincts, and even their convictions in certain matters, may not coincide with our own; but we can thank God for them and at times be inspired and challenged by their example. In the end, however, our focus must remain on Jesus himself. "Keep following me." Jesus alone is our Master; to him we belong, to him we must give account.[1]

We are to live our lives, as the writer of Hebrews said, with our eyes fixed firmly on Jesus (Heb. 12:2).

---

1. Bruce Milne, *The Message of John: Here Is Your King!*, The Bible Speaks Today Series (Downers Grove, Ill.: InterVarsity Press, 1993), p. 319.

Chapter 16

Many Other Signs . . . Many Other Things

John 20:30–31; 21:24–25

The End.

With those two words the novelist waves good-bye to the reader. If the book is good, it's a sorrowful parting, and the book is reluctantly closed with a sigh. If the tale has been compelling, the reader walks away from the book a changed person.

When one has finished reading the seventh and final volume of C. S. Lewis' *The Chronicles of Narnia,* it is just such a parting. But the story's end doesn't leave us pining so much for an eighth volume as it creates within us a yearning to be somehow infused into the story itself . . . to be a part of the group and a part of the grand adventure that awaits. Listen to Lewis draw the reader in as he concludes his story.

> And as He spoke He no longer looked to them like a lion; but the things that began to happen after that were so great and beautiful that I cannot write them. And for us this is the end of all the stories, and we can most truly say that they all lived happily ever after. But for them it was only the beginning of the real story. All their life in this world and all their adventures in Narnia had only been the cover and the title page: now at last they were beginning Chapter One of the Great Story, which no one on earth has read: which goes on for ever: in which every chapter is better than the one before.[1]

With these words, the author says good-bye. And with the words covered in this chapter, our good friend John bids us farewell. It is a tearful parting of author and reader; for the Gospel has been, quite literally, the greatest story ever told.

As we wave good-bye, a yearning wells up inside us—a yearning to be infused into that epic drama as an active participant. As we stand to give our ovations, we long to leave our cushioned seats and take our place on stage with the cast—to be a part of that courageous group and a part of the adventure on which they are about to embark.

1. C. S. Lewis, *The Last Battle* (New York, N.Y.: Macmillan Publishing Co., 1956), pp. 183–84.

I. The Signs He Performed

By the time John writes his Gospel, the end of the first century is near. Some sixty years have passed since Jesus died—a long time to linger over the memories of His life. With an eye for specific details that would substantiate his purpose, John has selected just the right shots for his scrapbook.

A. Stated facts. According to John's own testimony, the account has been selective, not exhaustive; the events are actual, not theoretical; the purpose is specific, not vague.

> Many other signs therefore Jesus also performed in the presence of the disciples, which are not written in this book; but these have been written that you may believe that Jesus is the Christ, the Son of God; and that believing you may have life in His name. (John 20:30–31)

B. Illustrated signs. John has strung together seven eventful pearls from the life of Christ, and the thread that runs through them all is His deity. The first took place when Jesus changed water into wine at a wedding in Cana (2:1–11). With this miracle, Jesus demonstrated His deity by proving Himself *Master over quality*. The second sign involved the healing of the official's son (4:46–54). Jesus effected the miracle from a distance of twenty miles, thereby proving Himself *Master over distance and space*. The third sign involved the healing of a man who had been sick for thirty-eight years (5:1–9). Jesus showed us in this miracle that there is no problem too old or too established that He can't solve, and in doing so, He proved Himself *Master over time*. In feeding the multitude (6:1–14), Jesus convincingly demonstrated that there is no obstacle too large or too widespread for Him to overcome. This established Him as *Master over quantity and size*. The fifth sign was found in 6:16–21 where Jesus walked on the water. The Lord quelled the disciples' fears with His presence and unquestioningly convinced them that He is *Master over nature*. In 9:1–7, Jesus gave sight to a man born blind, thus showing Himself as *Master over misfortune*. The final and most climactic sign involved raising Lazarus from the dead (chap. 11), dramatically proving Himself to be *Master over death*. In each of these seven miracles, Jesus demonstrated absolute control over all facets of life in which we humans exert such little control.

Opportunity Knocking

From time to time great opportunities knock on the doors of our lives—opportunities to exercise faith. But

they usually come disguised as impossibilities. The only
solution to these impossibilities is to introduce them to
the Master of the house—the Master who rules over
wind and waves, life and death, heaven and earth.

Do you have an impossible situation beating down
your door? That knock may sound threatening, but it's
really the knock of opportunity—an opportunity to be
stretched . . . and to grow!

II. The Things He Did

Jesus not only stunned the world with incredible accomplishments
that demonstrated true deity, but He served the world with incredible acts that displayed true humanity as well. John notes this at
the conclusion of his book.

This is the disciple who bears witness of these things,
and wrote these things; and we know that his witness
is true.

And there are also many other things which Jesus
did, which if they were written in detail, I suppose that
even the world itself would not contain the books which
were written. (21:24–25)

A. Viewed historically. In the many things Jesus did, He exhib-
ited humility (13:3–5, 12–15), identified with our needs (14:1,
25–27; 16:1, 31–33), submitted to death (17:1–5; chaps.
18–19), and demonstrated lasting friendship to the disciples
(chap. 21). Even after His work on earth was finished, Jesus
lingered long enough to stabilize those relationships He had
built over the last three and a half years. He is not a distant
deity but a friend who stays closer than a brother. He visited
the disciples while they were fishing . . . invited them to
breakfast . . . accepted and encouraged Peter . . . and ral-
lied the troops with a "Follow Me!" reveille. His loyalty and
love for those eleven men never waned. And the effects of
what Jesus did for the disciples lived on, long after He was
gone, inspiring them to follow in His steps. Peter later
preached to the same crowds responsible for Jesus' death and
founded the church in Jerusalem. Years later, he was crucified
upside down. James was faithful to the end and was finally
beheaded. Philip labored for Christ until A.D. 54, when he was
scourged, imprisoned, and then crucified. Matthew served in
Parthis and Ethiopia until A.D. 60, when he was bound, covered
with asphalt and oil, and burned to death. Andrew became an
itinerant preacher, ministering especially to the Scythians who

inhabited what we now know as Russia. He, too, was mercilessly beaten and crucified. And Thomas. Remember him? The one we've branded as "the doubter"? He was a missionary to India, where he was imprisoned, tortured by pagan priests, and stabbed to death with a spear. The others as well all died violent deaths in service to their Lord. John was the last to die. He founded churches at cities in a land we know today as Turkey—Smyrna, Pergamum, Sardis, Philadelphia, Laodicea, and Thyatira. He also ministered long at Ephesus, where he probably wrote his Gospel and his letters. From there he was ordered to Rome, where he was cast into a caldron of boiling oil. He narrowly escaped death, bearing the scars of that ordeal to his dying day. Banished for a time to the tiny island of Patmos, he there penned the book of Revelation.[2] So deep was their love for the Savior, who laid down His life for them, these loyal friends thought nothing of returning the sacrifice.[3]

B. **Viewed personally.** When Jesus is the subject of our study, all the books in all the world's libraries wouldn't be able to finish the story of His life. When Jesus is the object of our love, our lives change dramatically, and there is no end to the beautiful story our lives can tell. It's one thing to go through a book like John; it's another thing to have the book go through you. It's one thing to have a grasp on John's message; it's quite another to have the message grasp you. As the Gospel of John draws to its denouement, we want Jesus to be not simply the subject of your study but the object of your love. And like the disciples, may you enter into the captivating, adventurous story of life with Christ. And may your story be truly great . . . one that goes on forever . . . in which every chapter is better than the one before!

Living Insights

"The End." Yes, it is the end of John's Gospel, but just as the Cross was not the end of Jesus, so the last verses of this book are not the end of Jesus' story. His story, you see, continues in each of us as we abide in Him, bear fruit for Him, and bring glory to Him

---

2. John's death is clouded in obscurity. Some sources say he died peacefully in Ephesus; others say he was hunted down, brutalized, and buried alive.

3. For more information on the deaths of the disciples, consult *Fox's Book of Martyrs,* by John Fox (Grand Rapids, Mich.: Zondervan Publishing House, 1967), pp. 1–5.

while we wait for His return and the full realization of His kingdom. That is, it continues in each of us who believe in Him.

Has John's Gospel achieved the purpose he set out for it in your life? Have you come to believe that Jesus Christ is God's only Son, whom He sent into the world so that anyone and everyone who would place their faith in Him would be spared judgment and receive eternal life? If you haven't yet, won't you do so now? What is there to gain by keeping the One who is life and who gives life at a distance? If you'd like, write down your prayer of belief in Jesus and put this day's date on it so you can always remember this turning point from darkness to light in your life.

_____

_____

_____

_____

_____

If you already belong to Christ, have you come to believe more deeply in Him through this study? In what ways?

_____

_____

_____

_____

What aspect of Jesus has touched you the most in this study of John's Gospel?

_____

_____

_____

_____

What has challenged you the most?

_____

What has changed you?

In what areas do you need to grow more?

John, our eyewitness to Christ, is a good guide into Jesus' heart. If you would like to travel further with him as you continue to live out Jesus' story, we heartily recommend his three letters—1, 2, and 3 John—as well as his vision of Jesus in His triumph: Revelation. The following commentaries are very reliable (and readable) companions: David Jackman, *The Message of John's Letters: Living in the Love of God*, The Bible Speaks Today Series (Downers Grove, Ill.: InterVarsity Press, 1988); Michael Wilcock, *The Message of Revelation: I Saw Heaven Opened*, The Bible Speaks Today Series (Downers Grove, Ill.: InterVarsity Press, 1975).

In the meantime, remember that Jesus is ever near you, ever guiding you, ever calling you home.

"Let not your heart be troubled; believe in God, believe also in Me. . . . I go and prepare a place for you, I will come again, and receive you to Myself; that where I am, there you may be also." (John 14:1, 3)

Amen, and Amen!

Books for Probing Further

"There they crucified Him, and with Him two other men, one on either side, and Jesus in between" (John 19:18).

> The cross stood
>   like a set of scales
>   silhouetted against the Jerusalem sky,
> Its upraised stanchion
>   balancing a crossbeam
>   where love and justice met,
>   where all humanity had been weighed—
>   and found wanting.
> It was there Jesus hung,
>   with outstretched arms,
>   yearning for the world's embrace.
> On either side hung two thieves,
>   teetering between life and death,
>   Heaven and Hell;
> Teetering, until one, at last,
>   reached out in faith:
>   "Remember me when You come into Your kingdom."
> It was the last kind word said to Jesus before He died,
>   spoken not by a religious leader,
>   nor by the disciple whom Christ loved,
>   nor even by His mother standing at His feet,
>   but by a common thief.
> And with the words
>   "Today you will be with Me in Paradise,"
>   that thief was lifted off those weighted scales
>   and into the waiting arms
>   of the Savior,
> And in His arms was carried
>   that day,
>   as promised,
>   into the Kingdom of God.
> And as they entered, all of Heaven cheered!

—Ken Gire

There is no greater story than the life of Christ. It is epic in all its proportions. Any other story, any other life, pales by comparison.

We hope these studies on the life of our Lord have brought you to the Cross, and to your knees. We hope you have seen the Savior a little more clearly, and, as a result, love Him more dearly and follow Him more nearly.

To help you keep your eyes fixed on Jesus, we recommend the following books.

I. Jesus Christ

Bruce, F. F. *Jesus: Lord and Savior.* The Jesus Library Series. Downers Grove, Ill.: InterVarsity Press, 1986.

Gire, Ken. *Intense Moments with the Savior.* Grand Rapids, Mich.: Zondervan Publishing House, 1994.

Magdalen, Margaret. *Jesus, Man of Prayer.* The Jesus Library Series. Downers Grove, Ill.: InterVarsity Press, 1987.

Miller, Calvin, ed. *The Book of Jesus: A Treasury of the Greatest Stories and Writings about Christ.* New York, N.Y.: Simon and Schuster, 1996.

II. The Holy Spirit

Gromacki, Robert. *The Holy Spirit: Who He Is, What He Does.* Swindoll Leadership Library. Nashville, Tenn.: Thomas Nelson/Word Publishing Group, 1999.

Walvoord, John F. *The Holy Spirit: A Comprehensive Study of the Person and Work of the Holy Spirit.* Grand Rapids, Mich.: Zondervan Publishing House, Academic and Professional Books, 1991.

III. Commentaries on John's Gospel

Barclay, William. *The Gospel of John.* Vols. 1 and 2. Rev. ed. The Daily Study Bible Series. Philadelphia, Pa.: Westminster Press, 1975.

Barton, Bruce B., Philip W. Comfort, David R. Veerman, and Neil Wilson. *John.* Life Application Bible Commentary Series. Wheaton, Ill.: Tyndale House Publishers, 1993.

Carson, D. A. *The Gospel according to John.* Grand Rapids, Mich.: William B. Eerdmans Publishing Co., 1991.

Milne, Bruce. *The Message of John: Here Is Your King!* The Bible Speaks Today Series. Downers Grove, Ill.: InterVarsity Press, 1993.

Morris, Leon. *The Gospel according to John.* Rev. ed. The New International Commentary on the New Testament Series. Grand Rapids, Mich.: William B. Eerdmans Publishing Co., 1995.

Newbigin, Lesslie. *The Light Has Come: An Exposition of the Fourth Gospel.* Grand Rapids, Mich.: William B. Eerdmans Publishing Co., 1982.

Tenney, Merrill C. *John: The Gospel of Belief.* 1976. Reprint, Grand Rapids, Mich.: William B. Eerdmans Publishing Co., 1989.

IV. Jesus' Crucifixion

Green, Michael. *The Empty Cross of Jesus.* The Jesus Library Series. Downers Grove, Ill.: InterVarsity Press, 1984.

Lloyd-Jones, D. Martyn. *The Cross.* Westchester, Ill.: Good News Publishers, Crossway Books, 1986.

Lucado, Max. *No Wonder They Call Him the Savior.* Portland, Ore.: Multnomah Press, 1986.

Morris, Leon. *The Cross of Jesus.* Grand Rapids, Mich.: William B. Eerdmans Publishing Co., 1988.

Radmacher, Earl. *Salvation.* Swindoll Leadership Library. Nashville, Tenn.: Word Books, 2000.

Smith, Wilbur, ed. *Jesus' Death.* Vol. 2 of *Great Sermons on Christ.* Grand Rapids, Mich.: Baker Book House, 1991.

Stott, John R. W. *The Cross of Christ.* Downers Grove, Ill.: InterVarsity Press, 1986.

V. Jesus' Resurrection

Marshall, Peter. *The First Easter.* Old Tappan, N.J.: Fleming H. Revell Co., Chosen Books, 1987.

Smith, Wilbur, ed. *Jesus' Resurrection.* Vol. 3 of *Great Sermons on Christ.* Grand Rapids, Mich.: Baker Book House, 1991.

Tenney, Merrill C. *The Reality of the Resurrection.* New York, N.Y.: Harper and Row, Publishers, 1963.

VI. Relationship with Jesus

Curtis, Brent, and John Eldredge. *The Sacred Romance: Drawing Closer to the Heart of God.* Nashville, Tenn.: Thomas Nelson Publishers, 1997.

Wright, N. T. *Following Jesus: Biblical Reflections on Discipleship.* Grand Rapids, Mich.: William B. Eerdmans Publishing Co., 1994.

Some of these books may be out of print and available only through a library. For those currently available, please contact your local Christian bookstore. Books by Charles R. Swindoll, as well as some books by other authors, may be obtained through Insight for Living.

Insight for Living also offers study guides on many books of the Bible, as well as on a variety of issues and biblical personalities. For more information, see the ordering instructions that follow and contact the office that serves you.

Notes

Notes

Notes

Notes

Ordering Information

Exalting Christ . . . The Lamb of God

If you would like to order additional study guides, purchase the cassette series that accompanies this guide, or request our product catalogs, please contact the office that serves you.

United States and International locations:

Insight for Living
Post Office Box 69000
Anaheim, CA 92817-0900
1-800-772-8888, 24 hours a day, seven days a week
(714) 575-5000, 8:00 A.M. to 4:30 P.M., Pacific time,
Monday to Friday

Canada:

Insight for Living Ministries
Post Office Box 2510
Vancouver, BC, Canada V6B 3W7
1-800-663-7639, 24 hours a day, seven days a week

Australia:

Insight for Living, Inc.
20 Albert Street
Blackburn, VIC 3130, Australia
Toll-free 1800-772-888 or (03) 9877-4277, 8:30 A.M. to 5:00 P.M.,
Monday to Friday

World Wide Web:

www.insight.org

Study Guide Subscription Program

Study guide subscriptions are available. Please call or write the office nearest you to find out how you can receive our study guides on a regular basis.